CAMBRIDGE   CONTEXTS IN LITERATURE

Natasha Distille

Post-Colonial Literature

Christopher O'Reilly

Series Editor: Adrian Barlow

CAMBRIDGE
UNIVERSITY PRESS

PUBLISHED BY THE PRESS SYNDICATE OF THE UNIVERSITY OF CAMBRIDGE
The Pitt Building, Trumpington Street, Cambridge, United Kingdom

CAMBRIDGE UNIVERSITY PRESS
The Edinburgh Building, Cambridge CB2 2RU, UK
40 West 20th Street, New York, NY 10011–4211, USA
10 Stamford Road, Oakleigh, VIC 3166, Australia
Ruiz de Alarcón 13, 28014 Madrid, Spain
Dock House, The Waterfront, Cape Town 8001, South Africa

http://www.cambridge.org

First published 2001

Printed in the United Kingdom at the University Press, Cambridge

Typefaces: Clearface and Mixage   *System:* QuarkXPress® 4.1

A catalogue record for this book is available from the British Library

ISBN 0 521 77554 X paperback

Prepared for publication by Gill Stacey
Designed by Tattersall Hammarling & Silk
Cover illustration: © Reuters/Popperfoto

Contents

Introduction

What is post-colonial literature?

It is sometimes easier to use the label 'post-colonial literature' than to state exactly what is meant by it. This is not just because 'post-colonial' means different things to different people, but because of the range of writing to which the label can be applied. It can be applied to sonnets written by a 19th-century Indian female poet, to a novel depicting life in Nigeria before the arrival of the British, to the productions of theatre workshops in South Africa and to the reggae and 'dub' beats of black British poetry. What do these very different kinds of writing have in common? Why might they be categorised as post-colonial literature?

One simple answer is that all the above writing has arisen out of experiences which result from contact with the British empire. In this sense, post-colonial literature is writing which reflects, in a great variety of ways, the effects of colonialism. This might include the enforced mass migrations of the slave trade, or the impact of colonialism upon indigenous societies, to name only two areas of focus. Post-colonial literature is a large topic.

Though post-colonial writing is clearly a response to empire, it should not, however, be defined purely against it. As 'post-' implies, it is also the literature written after the end of formal colonial rule. The British retreat from empire after the Second World War and the gaining of independence by the vast majority of its colonies (those, such as the Falkland Islands, which are still colonies, are so by choice) has meant that, particularly in what has been termed the 'developing' or 'Third World', new conflicts and power struggles have arisen; the television screens of Europe often show pictures of ethnic conflict or famine, and in some countries corruption has come to characterise much post-independence politics. Internal conflict has been one legacy of colonialism, particularly in countries such as India or Nigeria where traditionally isolated or conflicting groups were brought within national boundaries created by colonialists. This is another context which informs the writing of post-colonial authors: the problems faced by independent countries and the lack of security and certainty in such a world. On one level, post-colonial literature is an expression of these crises as well as a testimony to those who resist them. In an important way, it also presents alternative perspectives of Third World countries to those presented on the television screens of the West.

Many might argue that it is a mistake to describe such a world as 'post-colonial'. Political independence has not necessarily brought economic freedom. Many countries are still economically dependent on the 'developed' world, produce cash-crops such as coffee or tobacco for multi-national companies that reap the profits, and are ruled by dictators supported by foreign aid. It can be argued that such a world is not post-colonial, but 'neo-colonial': though the obvious signs of empire may be gone, the populations of such countries have not gained the freedom that they hoped would come after independence. By 1966 increasingly oppressive regimes or military rule could be seen in Kenya, Uganda, Ghana and Nigeria, to name only four countries.

Post-colonial literature should be clearly distinguished from colonial literature. For the purposes of this book, 'colonial writing' is writing produced by authors who belong to the colonising power (white writing about India, Africa or the Caribbean) and written before independence in the relevant region. Colonial writing also comes in many shapes and forms; it covers a large time frame, from the 16th to 20th centuries, and colonial writers are certainly not uniform in their depiction or opinion of empire. Though it is only possible to include a small amount of colonial writing in this book, what can be included is there to provide key examples of its kind and to be seen in relation to the writing of post-colonial authors. Colonial writing can act as a backdrop highlighting the particular concerns of post-colonial authors, who have, in various ways, responded to it.

'Colonial writing'

The label 'post-colonial' demands a shift in focus, away from British literature (literature produced by British writers) to world literatures in English. Whereas it would have once seemed impossible to separate Britain and British attitudes from great writing in English, post-colonial literature questions the importance of both 'Britishness' and 'Englishness'. Perhaps the prominence of post-colonial literature reflects the changing nature of British society itself, which is now multi-cultural. Furthermore, whereas English literature was once exported throughout the empire, through schools and colleges, now the writing from former colonies is being exported to Britain. In the words of the Indian novelist, Salman Rushdie: 'The Empire writes back to the centre.' This book attempts to deal with the implications of that shift.

The purpose and scope of the book

The book discusses the key issues relating to post-colonial writing, providing a sense of the historical and cultural background which has shaped the subject.

Since post-colonial writers often respond to particular historical events, post-colonial literature is intimately entwined with the contexts in which it is written; indeed, part of the purpose of this book is to provide a sense of the various contexts of post-colonial literature. This is certainly not to argue that writing is a mere by-product of history (the written or performed word is always the primary focus), but to show how different writers are influenced by, respond to and perhaps shape the societies in which they live.

as is all literature

The global nature of post-colonial literature means that the reader needs to be aware of a variety of contexts. Because of the influence of migration and the availability of global travel, writers may not belong to or identify with one geographical region, but cross both regional and cultural boundaries through their writing. Though there are issues, such as the use of the English language, which are common across the globe, much post-colonial writing reflects the concerns of the particular region in which it is written. In addition to this, the British empire was a far from uniform operation, differing greatly in the various regions. For these reasons, Part 1: Approaching post-colonial writing, which offers an overview, is devoted to both 'Transcultural writing' and to particular geographical regions: India, Africa and the Caribbean.

Owing to the limitations of space, this book does not cover writing from New Zealand, Australia or Canada. These (along with South Africa) were 'white dominions' with greater control over their own internal affairs and foreign policy, and though their writers faced some similar problems to those from Britain's 'colonies', they require a distinctive introduction of their own. The colonies, however, are linked together because of the extent to which they were prevented from managing their own affairs, and by the fact that, until they gained independence, power was in the hands of a white élite responsible to the government in London.

Much of the focus of this book is about how authors from subjugated peoples and races have come to take the English language, taught to them initially by their colonial masters, and have used it for their own literary purposes, transforming it in the process. This book seeks to provide an introduction to why, how and when this occurred.

How the book is organised

Part 1: Approaching post-colonial writing

Part 1 provides an introduction to the main features of post-colonial writing, key post-colonial authors and the development of post-colonial literature within specific geographical contexts.

Part 2: Approaching the texts

Part 2 raises essential issues which need to be kept in mind when reading post-colonial literature, and is designed to provoke close, critical reading.

Part 3: Texts and extracts

This part offers an anthology of writing, which will be referred to in the other sections and which can be used as the basis of tasks and assignments. It is organised regionally, according to the place represented in the passage.

Part 4: Critical approaches

An introduction to post-colonial criticism, this section emphasises the importance of recognising different ways of writing about colonial and post-colonial literature and provides an introduction to the central critical concepts and vocabulary used. There is also guidance on how to write about colonial and post-colonial literature, as well as writing about established English texts from a post-colonial perspective.

Part 5: Resources

This includes a reading list and other resources, providing a list of the primary texts used in this book, as well as useful guides to the subject as a whole and the regions under discussion. It also includes a selection of useful internet sites.

There is a glossary which lists and defines the critical terms which, when used, appear in bold type.

There are tasks and assignments, for individual or group work, in Parts 1, 2, and 4.

1 | Approaching post-colonial writing

- What are the main characteristics of post-colonial literature?

- How has post-colonial writing developed in different geographical, cultural and political contexts?

- How have individual authors responded to key historical and cultural developments?

Transcultural writing

First and foremost, post-colonial writing is an international genre. It would be a mistake to imply that all authors can be neatly tied, either culturally or personally, to their countries of origin. Indeed, a sense of origin or belonging is often conspicuously absent. Furthermore, the setting and scope of much post-colonial writing is international rather than local in focus. Deciding whether a work should be placed in a local or international context is a key issue when approaching post-colonial writing.

V.S. Naipaul and Salman Rushdie: the problem of context

Look at the following extract from the novel *A Bend in the River* (1979) by the writer V.S. Naipaul; the narrator, Salim, a man of East African Muslim descent, is making observations about the life of immigrants and refugees in London.

> They traded in the middle of London as they traded in the middle of Africa. The goods travelled a shorter distance, but the relationship of the trader to his goods remained the same. In the streets of London I saw these people, who were like myself, as from a distance. I saw the young girls selling packets of cigarettes at midnight, seemingly imprisoned in their kiosks, like puppets in a puppet theatre. They were cut off from the life of the great city where they had come to live, and I wondered about the pointlessness of their own hard life, the pointlessness of their difficult journey.

As soon as the reader begins to consider where to place the passage geographically, questions arise. Should the passage be seen as being written from the perspective of Salim's personal background? Should it be seen within the context of London, where the passage is set, even though the narrator and people described are outsiders to that city?

To complicate matters further, the author was born in Trinidad of Hindu Indian descent, but has lived most of his adult life away from the place of his birth, much of it travelling in Africa and India. Is it not possible to argue that the writing could be seen as Caribbean, Indian or African, even English, depending where the reader chooses to place emphasis?

Displacement and rootlessness

These questions highlight how difficult it can be to place writers and texts within a specific context. Indeed, for some, displacement is the key feature of the post-colonial world. Its effects, both cultural and psychological, are central themes in post-colonial literature.

▶ Look again at the passage and consider how displacement is depicted. What particular words, phrases or sentences highlight this?

Writers who do not fit neatly into any particular area can be described as 'transcultural' in the sense that they live and write 'across' national and cultural boundaries. One characteristic feature of such writing is a sense of rootlessness, though this may not always be immediately obvious. Such dislocation raises all sorts of interesting questions about the subject of post-colonial writing, and the way in which it relates to its context.

'trans cultural'

Transcultural writing reminds the reader that writers do not always have a rich sense of culture to draw from like a well, and that their relationship with the culture or nation of their birth or heritage can often be problematic. On one level, such writing challenges the idea that national and cultural identities can be easily defined, and that individuals fit neatly into such categories.

Near the beginning of *A Bend in the River,* Salim describes his origins:

> Africa was my home, had been the home of my family for centuries. But we came from the East coast, and that made the difference. The coast was not truly African. It was an Arab-Indian-Persian-Portugese place, and we who lived there were really people of the Indian Ocean. True Africa was at our back. Many miles of scrub and desert separated us from the up-country people; we looked east to the lands with which we traded – Arabia, India, Persia. These were also the lands of our ancestors. But we could no longer say that we were

Arabians or Indians or Persians; when we compared ourselves with these people, we felt like people of Africa.

Naipaul has created a narrator who, despite the distinctiveness of his position, is caught between cultures. Even though his family have actually lived in Africa 'for centuries', they are 'really people of the Indian Ocean'. However, even that is not secure; when they compare themselves with Arabians, Indians or Persians, they 'felt like people of Africa'.

Living between cultures

Though the details may be different, the sense of living between cultures can be seen to reflect Naipaul's own predicament. Naipaul is the grandson of indentured (contracted) labourers who were brought to the Caribbean, in his case Trinidad, from India to supply cheap labour on plantations after the abolition of slavery in the 19th century. As such he was born into a family which still practised Indian, Hindu rituals, but was thousands of miles from the source of those rituals. The Port of Spain in which Naipaul grew up had Indian, black, American and English communities.

It is far from coincidental that Naipaul is equally a travel writer and a writer of fiction. His travel writing is as much an exploration into history and the relationship between the past and the present as it is about scenes, occurrences and experiences. In *Finding the Centre* (1984), Naipaul has written about the process of writing and his motivations for travel, specifically in the Ivory Coast, West Africa. One of the aspects he focuses on is meeting people:

> But the people I found, the people I was attracted to were not unlike myself. They were trying to find order in their world, looking for the centre ...

▶ Given that Naipaul is predominantly an exile, why might 'order' and a 'centre' be so important for him? What might they offer on a psychological level?

The above statements by Naipaul reflect a key problem for many writers living in the post-colonial world. That is, how to make sense of and represent a world which may not seem ordered or meaningful. This does not necessarily mean denying uncertainty and doubt, but incorporating it into the picture.

The process of writing across cultures may affect the actual writing process itself. Reflecting on the experience of writing his novel, *Miguel Street* (1959), Naipaul relates how he came to recreate his native Port of Spain while writing in London. Consider this extract from *Finding the Centre*:

The first sentence was true. The second was invention. But together – to me, the writer – they had done something extraordinary. Though they had left out everything – the setting, the historical time, the racial and social complexities of the people concerned – they had suggested it all; they had created the world of the street …

So, that afternoon in the Langham Hotel, Port of Spain memories, disregarded until then, were simplified and transformed … When I began to write about Bogart's street I began to sink into a tract of experience I hadn't before contemplated as a writer. Half of the writer's work though is the discovery of his subject. And a problem for me was that my life had been varied … Trying to make a beginning as a writer I didn't know where to focus.

The experience of exile gave him the clarity and distance to manage the material.

However, exile presents different problems for different post-colonial authors, and may affect their writing in different ways. In his essay 'Imaginary Homelands' (1992), Salman Rushdie reflects upon the process of writing about India while living in London (because of Rushdie's own sense of himself as an Indian writer, a more detailed introduction to his work is included in the section on India, pages 24–26):

> It may be that writers in my position, exiles or emigrants or expatriates, are haunted by some sense of loss, some urge to reclaim, to look back even at the risk of being mutated into pillars of salt. But if we do look back, we must also do so in the knowledge – which gives rise to profound uncertainties – that our physical alienation means that we will not be capable of reclaiming precisely the thing that was lost; that we will, in short, create fictions, not actual cities or villages, but invisible ones, imaginary homelands, Indias of the mind …

[margin notes: exile + distance from subject matter; loss]

This passage emphasises a fundamental issue when approaching all writing, not just transcultural works: the position of the author, whether geographical or cultural, and how that affects the way in which the subject is perceived and represented.

Authenticity

In addition to this, the extract raises another essential issue: 'authenticity'. To what extent can a piece of writing be seen to reflect or convey truly a particular event or moment? On the one hand, post-colonial literature offers us fictions (such as Rushdie's 'Indias of the mind') which have been constructed and selected, and are not accurate, complete **representations** of the world, no matter how convincing they might seem. However, there is a sense in which writing reflects the world, as in the extracts from *A Bend in the River* above.

Post-colonial literature often works in an area between what is fact and fiction, or what is history and literature.

Michael Ondaatje: the search for identity

the personal – "identity"

The writing of Michael Ondaatje highlights the subjective, personal element of the post-colonial world. Originally from Sri Lanka (then Ceylon), his roots are of mixed Dutch, Tamil and Sinhalese elements. Educated in England, he eventually settled in Canada. A sense of the transcultural informs much of his work, whether in the form of migration, international displacement or the personal search for his family's past. Above all, his work heightens a sense of a world which is not ordered and fixed, but relative, composed of various perspectives and histories.

In Ondaatje's novel, *The English Patient* (1992), the reader is given an insight into the highly individual, but entwined histories of the main characters. Though much of the novel is set in Italy at the end of the Second World War, action also takes place in Canada, North Africa, England and India. All of the four main characters are removed from their culture of origin, and the nature of their experiences means that they become entwined in lives of those from cultures other than their own. Though the sense of place and history is global in dimension, Ondaatje focuses on the intimate, inner world of each character.

It is significant that for much of the novel the central character of *The English Patient* is nameless and featureless, distinctive features having been burnt in a plane crash, his identity a mystery. Even when Carravagio (another character) reveals his identity as an Hungarian spy, Count Almasy, the nurse, Hana, rejects this as the past and unimportant. The English patient has assimilated Englishness to the degree that he can no longer be distinguished as Hungarian or English. Moreover, the novel is set at a time of chaos in Europe and at the beginning of the decline of European empires. A sense of the disintegration of formal order, and the need to create clarity in the world, is conveyed in the following passage:

> The Bedouin were keeping me alive for a reason. I was useful, you
> see. Someone there had assumed I had a skill when my plane crashed
> in the desert. I am a man who can recognise an unnamed town by its
> skeletal shape on a map. I have always had information like a sea in
> me. I am a person who if left alone in someone's home walks to the
> bookcase, pulls down a volume and inhales it. So history enters us. I
> knew maps of the sea floor, maps that depict weaknesses in the

shield of the earth, charts painted on skin that contain the various routes of the Crusades.

So I knew their place before I crashed among them, knew when Alexander had traversed it in an earlier age, for this cause or that greed. I knew the customs of nomads besotted with silk or wells ... There were continual drownings, tribes suddenly made historical with sand across their gasp.

In the desert it is easy to lose a sense of demarcation. When I came out of the air and into the desert, into those troughs of yellow, all I kept thinking was, I must build a raft ... I must build a raft.

▶ In what ways might the passage seem 'transcultural'? How does Ondaatje link a sense of history with a sense of place and personal experience?

Perhaps the loss of easy 'demarcation' characterises the post-colonial world. The colonial spy, a man of knowledge and maps, finds himself in the ever-shifting desert. Human civilisation and history are seen in terms of quest and migration, of change, of survival or 'drownings'.

Do post-colonial writers provide us with maps, however imperfect, which represent a world that is continually changing? Maps which are incomplete, cultural and psychological, as much as physical, but which still give some insight?

po-co
writing as
incomplete
maps

The theme of mapping countries and experiences across cultural boundaries is a key aspect of *Running in the Family* (1983), which is based on Ondaatje's return visits to Sri Lanka. Throughout this work , the reader is aware of a world being reconstructed. In the section 'Aunts', he writes:

How I have used them ... They knit the story together, each memory a wild thread in the sarong. They lead me through their dark rooms crowded with various kinds of furniture – teak, rattan, calamander, bamboo – their voices whispering over tea, cigarettes, distracting me from the tale with their long bony arms, which move over the table like the stretched feet of storks. I would love to photograph this.

A sense of the book's make-up can be gleaned from knowing that it includes historical detail, photographs and extracts from conversations. Alongside these are placed translations of 5th-century poetry, diary extracts and Ondaatje's own poetry. As with *The English Patient,* the map we are given is a composition of possible perspectives, so that the fictional, imaginary aspect is emphasised. Towards the end, addressing his dead parents, he states, 'But the book again is incomplete. In the end all your children move along the scattered acts and memories with no more clues.' When acknowledging the help of others, Ondaatje writes:

> While these names may give an air of authenticity, I must confess that
> the book is not a history but a portrait or "gesture" …

fiction
map

reality
territory

The reader is asked not to mistake fiction for reality, the map for the territory. This is a key point when reading not just transcultural writing, but post-colonial literature in general.

India

India was the first of Britain's colonies to gain independence. In August 1947, the modern political state of India was created, alongside Pakistan. Only 50 years previously, at the height of British rule in India (the Raj), such an event would have seemed impossible. India had been the 'jewel' in the imperial crown. It had occupied a prominent place in the imagination of writers, scholars and politicians for over 300 years. Furthermore, culturally and politically, Britain had made a great impact on Indian society.

However, the British influence is only one force to have shaped Indian society. Much Indian writing in English reflects deeper cultural and religious traditions, most prominently those of Hinduism and Islam. When thinking about the broader context of Indian writing, what becomes clear is not so much a set of recent events, but a sense of these deep cultural traditions. Often, to read the literature itself is to come into contact with these, whether they are presented faithfully, critically or humorously.

The place of the English language in India is a complex and interesting one. Because of its historical association with the British, many thought it would die out after independence; instead, English has been adopted and adapted by Indian writers for their own purposes. But before discussing how this has occurred, it might be useful to outline some of the key cultural effects of British rule in India, as these helped to create a tradition of Indian writing in English.

The historical and cultural context: British rule and Indian culture

British involvement in India began as early as the 16th century, most notably through the East India Company, which was granted a Royal Charter by Queen Elizabeth I in 1600. The initial trading for spices and textiles can be seen as part of Britain's first major phase of imperial expansion. Clive of India's victory at Plassey, in 1757, is generally taken as the moment from which British rule in India can be measured. Previously, Calcutta had been taken by the Nawab Siraj-ud-daula. Clive retook the city and defeated him at Plassey, gaining immense property, revenue and asserting British dominance in the area. But at this point British cultural interference was minimal: so long as revenue was paid to the British, Muslim nawabs and Hindu princes retained the trappings of their accustomed lifestyle. Very few Indians learnt English and there was no formal education for this.

Effective British rule was, however, only possible because of the large number of Orientalists (scholars specialising in the study of the East), who joined and were trained by the Company. With the help of local scribes, linguists and priests, they were able to master the indigenous languages. Their interests were wide, covering law, literature, religion, indeed the whole spectrum of Indian culture. It is possible to see the British acquisition of India as paralleled by the acquisition of a range of Indian art and culture, and the gathering and collating of 'knowledge' about indigenous customs. What advantages, either psychological or practical, would this knowledge give the Company as they began to take control?

Macaulay's 'Minute on Education'

After the suppression of the Indian Mutiny of 1857, British rule became more tightly controlled. In 1858 the East India Company was abolished and India placed directly under the authority of the Crown. In 1876 Queen Victoria was declared 'Empress of India'. Colleges were established where instruction in English was compulsory and the curriculum European. The reasons for this decision can be traced back to Thomas B. Macaulay's 1835 'Minute on Education':

Macaulay

> All parties seem to be agreed on one point, that the dialects commonly spoken among the natives of this part of India contain neither literary nor scientific information, and are, moreover, so rude that, until they are enriched with some quarter, it will not be possible to translate any valuable work into them ... I am quite ready to take Oriental learning at the valuation of the Orientalists themselves. I have never found one among them who would deny that a single shelf of a good European library was worth the whole native literature of India and Arabia ... We must at present do our best to form a class of interpreters between us and the millions whom we govern; a class of persons Indian in blood and colour, but English in taste, in opinions, in morals and in intellect.

Crucially, the establishment of these colleges led to the creation of an English-educated, and predominantly Hindu, élite, who would be critical of both their own religious orthodoxies, such as the **caste system** and child brides, and of British rule. Most importantly, a British-style education linked Indian writers to literary traditions of the West, as well as their native culture. Writing in English, Indians

English education

made contact with an audience in Europe as well as in India. This dual audience forms the readership of much Indian writing in English today.

The growth of Indian nationalism

The 20th century saw radical changes in Indian politics which were to affect, in different ways, the key writers of the period. Various factors intensified anti-British feeling across all levels of society in India. The Indian Congress (established in 1885 to put Indian concerns to the British government) became increasingly frustrated. Their reasoned petitions were being ignored. Indians educated at Oxford, Cambridge and London were still excluded from positions of responsibility within the Indian Civil Service. Indian politicians were not consulted about India's entry into the First World War. There was a growing sense of social injustice and exploitation as industrial workers, particularly in Bombay, organised themselves into unions and were influenced by communist ideas.

The massacre at Amritsar

The British responded in ways which outraged Indians. The Rowlatt Acts (1919) made the sale of anti-imperialist literature illegal and the inciting of *hartals* (strikes) was outlawed. It was in response to these oppressive measures that protestors began peaceful demonstrations in Amritsar, in the Punjab. On April 13th, 379 unarmed, peaceful demonstrators, including women and children, were killed and 1200 wounded, under orders by Brigadier Dyer. After an act of such brutality, the moral injustice of the Raj became clearer, as did the fact that the British would not relinquish India unless they absolutely had to.

Mohandas Karamchand Gandhi (1869–1948)

Gandhi was by far the most influential and visionary figure of the independence movement. Though he never held any official office within Congress, he effectively turned the party into a mass political movement. His ideals and his influence created a whole culture of resistance to the British, which permeated the work of the main writers of the time.

Gandhi's political and spiritual ideals were inextricably linked. He became known as *Mahatma* meaning 'Great Soul'. His simple hand-spun shawl and loincloth became a symbol of integrity and dignity in the face of Western decadence and materialism. His insistence on *ahimsa* (non-violence) and his development of *satyagraha* (passive resistance), meaning 'truth-force', as a means of challenging the moral authority of the state, required great restraint and self-discipline on the part of volunteers. He was well aware that violence would weaken India's moral position. It could easily degenerate into chaos and fighting between Hindus and Muslims, which it increasingly did.

He was, however, a controversial figure. Modern socialists such as Jawaharlal Nehru (1880–1964) were often frustrated by his idiosyncratic rule and by the policy of passive resistance. Nehru, who was to become Prime Minister in 1947, stood for a modern, industrial India rather than Gandhi's ideal of small, self-sufficient communities. Communist activity also became more united in the 1930s, as a result of the increased suffering caused by the Great Depression, which was a world-wide economic crisis. The number of strikers doubled to 220,000 from 1932 to 1934.

▶ How do you think these political developments were likely to shape the concerns of writers during this period? How would they be different from those of the previous century?

Pre-independence literature: the development of the Indian novel

The three principal novelists of the period are Mulk Raj Anand, Raja Rao and R.K. Narayan. Each of these have responded in different ways to the political and cultural developments of the 'Gandhi era'.

Mulk Raj Anand

Anand, son of a coppersmith father and peasant mother, was born in 1905 on India's North West frontier. It has been said that his working class origins gave him real empathy with India's poor. He was educated at Punjab, London and Cambridge universities. He lived for a time at Gandhi's *ashram,* a social and spiritual community, where he found the insight and inspiration necessary to complete the novel *Untouchable* (1935). Indeed, Gandhi advised Anand on approaching this subject. Both *Untouchable* and his second novel, *Coolie* (1936), are protest novels: they speak out against the injustices of society and give a voice to those that have none.

Anand viewed his writing as part of the process of reforming Indian society. He saw his novels as creating new heroic characters to replace the heroes of the traditional Hindu epics and *puranas* ('Ancient Tales' about gods, kings or noble families).

▶ Anand's novels have also been called social **realist** or documentary novels. After reading the extract from *Coolie* (Part 3, pages 71–73), consider what these terms might mean.

▶ In an article entitled 'The sources of protest in my novels', Anand stated: 'Renaissance is the cue for all human passion, the freedom to grow, ever to higher consciousness.' How would you express this in your own words? How might those sentiments reflect the broader developments of the time?

While much of the novel *Untouchable* reflects the personal and psychological experiences of the untouchables Bakha, Sohini and their father, its ending reflects national debates concerning the issues of untouchability. Both the Salvation Army missionary and Gandhi seem to offer little hope to Bakha; though he is pleased that both Jesus and Gandhi wish to welcome untouchables as equals, the missionary cannot explain to him who Jesus is. Gandhi, though seeming to echo the pangs of his own heart, does not provide any effective solutions. The boy returns to the poverty of his home still in the same position as earlier that morning.

From today's perspective, it is difficult to appreciate how revolutionary the novel was. At the time, the publishers only agreed to print *Untouchable* if the British novelist, E.M. Forster (1879–1970), wrote a preface defending it. Forster had written critically about the Raj in his novel *A Passage to India* (1924). Anand sent a copy of the manuscript to Forster, who gave critical praise and offered help to get the book published. In the preface, Forster justifies the subject matter, while mocking English and Indian sensibilities about it. Despite this, most British debate centred around whether the book was 'dirty' or 'clean', and many reviews were hostile. The following lines are taken from the novel:

> He must have had immense pent-up resources lying deep in his body, for he rushed along with considerable skill and alacrity from one doorless latrine to another, cleaning, brushing, pouring phenoil. 'What a dextrous workman!' the onlooker would have said. And though his job was dirty, he remained comparatively clean. He didn't even soil his sleeves handling the commodes, sweeping and scrubbing them.

▶ Why might the need to break social and literary taboos be an important part of Indian writing, both pre- and post-independence? How might the realism of Anand's work be a means of reforming attitudes within Indian society?

Raja Rao

Raja Rao was born in 1909 into a high caste Brahmin family in Mysore State; he was one of the first Indian writers to 'appropriate' English so that it might become a medium for authentic Indian expression. In the foreword to his novel *Kanthapura* (1938), he wrote:

> The telling has not been easy. One has to convey in a language that is not one's own the spirit that is one's own. One has to convey the various shades and omissions of a certain thought-movement that looks maltreated in an alien language ... We cannot write like the English. We should not. ... Our method of expression has to therefore be a dialect which will sometimes prove to be as distinctive or

colourful as the Irish or the American … The tempo of Indian life must be infused into our English expression …

Set in rural Kanthapura, Rao's book is a testament to Gandhian politics; the novel's hero Moorthy is a Gandhi figure, teaching *pariahs* (untouchables), fasting in order to achieve *ahimsa*, suffering imprisonment, organising boycotts and *satyagraha* demonstrations (see page 18 above).

▶ Read the extract from *Kanthapura* (Part 3, pages 73–74), which is narrated by an elderly woman, and then reflect on the following questions.

• How do you think Rao's use of a particularly Indian English might relate to the novel's subject?

• Why do you think Rao chose his narrator to be an elderly woman of the village?

• What traditions, other than English, is he linking himself to?

R.K. Narayan

R.K. Narayan was born in 1906 into a high caste Madras Brahmin family. He is India's most longstanding and prolific novelist. His work spans the period of nationalist politics in the 1930s and the violence and corruption of the post-independence era. It is nearly all set in the imaginary town of Malgudi. Unlike Anand and Rao, Narayan has not explicitly dramatised the nationalist cause; he has said that he felt limited by the political expectations on writers during the pre-independence years, and that he preferred to concentrate on 'atmosphere, psychological factors, the crisis in the individual soul'. His main novels of this period – *Swami and Friends* (1935), *The Bachelor of Arts* (1937) and *The English Teacher* (1945) – deal with growing up and adulthood in Southern India.

Though perhaps not so radical as Rao in his **appropriation** of English, Narayan is part of the process, which, in his own word, is an 'Indianisation' of English. For Narayan, the language fulfilled its purpose by 'conveying unambiguously the thought and acts of a set of personalities' (his characters). This highlights an important aspect of post-colonial literature: conveying experience in a language which is foreign to the writer's culture.

Narayan communicates the subtleties of thought and feeling in his main characters, and the conventions of the high caste world they inhabit. Hindu customs, rituals and conventions, such as arranging a marriage in *The Bachelor of Arts,* or the cremation of the teacher's wife, Susila, in *The English Teacher*, are part of the fabric of his novels. The following passage is taken from *The Bachelor of Arts*:

So the first courtesies were exchanged between the families. As Chandran looked at the small piece of paper on which the horoscope was drawn, his heart bubbled over with joy. He noticed that the corners of the paper were touched with saffron – a mark of auspiciousness. So they had fully realised that it was an auspicious undertaking. Did not that fact indicate that they approved of this bridegroom and were anxious to secure him? ...

Chandran was happy the whole of the next day; but his mother constantly checked his exuberance: 'Chandran, you must not think that the only thing now to be settled is the date of the marriage. God helping, all the difficulties will be solved, but there are yet a number of preliminaries to be settled. First, our astrologer must tell us if your horoscope can be matched with the girl's; and then I don't know what their astrologer will say. Let us hope it will be for the best. After that, they must come and invite us to see the girl.'

In Narayan's work, the British presence is most strongly felt through the Albert Mission College, which embodies Macaulay's ideals. The Indian protagonists, Chandran and Krishnan, both reject the rote learning and mechanical fact cramming of the English syllabus: Chandran for the space to 'synthesise' his own thoughts and ideas, and Krishnan to partake in an 'educational experiment' at a primary school. (See the extract from *The English Teacher* in Part 3, pages 74–75.)

▶ After reading the extract on pages 74–75, reflect on the following.

• Even if Narayan's novels do not take any obviously political stance, how might this kind of writing be seen as part of a process of cultural reassertion?

• What do you think are the advantages of this non-politically motivated writing?

▶ The Indian critic K.R.S. Iyengar said that writing in English, after restoring national self-respect, had two further stages: one, identifying 'with the common people'; two, 'bridging the gap between East and West'. To what extent do you think that the novelists you are reading fulfil these functions?

The historical and cultural context: independence and partition

The events surrounding Indian independence have had a profound effect on modern Indian writers and Indian society as a whole. Indian novelists were not confronted with Gandhi's ideal of a tolerant, secular country, but one which saw increased religious extremism and violence (Gandhi himself was assassinated by a Hindu extremist in January 1948 after trying to curb hatred between Hindus, Sikhs and Muslims in Delhi).

At the heart of this conflict lay the emphasis on communal politics (politics based on religion) as independence became inevitable. The Muslim League (founded in 1906 to represent Muslim interests) feared being overwhelmed by the predominantly Hindu Congress Party. The League claimed to speak for all Muslims and, under the leadership of Muhammad Ali Jinnah (1876–1948), demanded a separate Muslim State, Pakistan. In order to achieve this, Muslims took 'direct action': in Bengal attacks by Muslims on Hindus and Sikhs, in August 1946, led to a series of reprisals and counterattacks, which left at least 4000 dead. There was rioting in Bombay and Bihar, where up to 7000 people were killed by October.

Though The Muslim League achieved their aims when Pakistan came into being on 15 August 1947, it was at a high price. Pakistan, meaning 'land of the pure' in Urdu (traditionally the language of the Islamic Moghul court), was created in two halves: West Pakistan by annexing the Western Provinces of the Punjab, Sind and Balukistan, and East Pakistan by annexing East Bengal. The cost in human suffering was immense: fearing religious violence and retribution, approximately 13 million people fled either into or out of the new states. By 1948, 180,000 people had been killed in the Punjab alone.

Indira Gandhi and the State of Emergency
Less than 35 years after India gained independence, the Prime Minister, Indira Gandhi (1917–1984), declared a State of Emergency and imposed martial law upon the country. Indira Gandhi, who was Nehru's granddaughter, had been accused and convicted of electoral fraud in 1975. Her response was to jail thousands of her opponents, even those in her own party. Newspapers were censored and those states not governed by the Congress Party came under direct rule from Delhi. Though the Emergency ended in 1977 and Indira Gandhi lost that election, it has left a deep mark on Indian writing. Not only were the ideals of democracy and free speech rebuked, but policies instigated during that time reflected a clinical contempt for the poor and underprivileged.

Perhaps the most controversial of these was the sterilisation programme enacted by her son, Sanjay Gandhi (1946–1980). As an attempt to curb India's increasing birth rate, 'incentives' (ranging from money to transistor radios) were offered to those men willing to undergo vasectomies. Such methods obviously exploited the needs of India's poor. To meet quotas, no consideration was given to the age or health of the men coerced into participating. There is also evidence of enforced sterilisations. The protests which broke out were used as an opportunity to enact further undemocratic policies. In Delhi, there were slum clearances and the removal of squatters as part of a process of 'beautification'.

Post-independence Indian writing
Since 1947 Indian writing in English has developed in a wide variety of styles and

represents a variety of perspectives. The authors and works discussed here reflect some of the key developments of this period, but certainly not all. Indeed, the sheer size of India, the world's largest democracy, with numerous religions and strong regional identities, is perhaps a reminder that Indian writing can only offer the reader perspectives on aspects of Indian life and politics. India is not one place or idea, but a multiplicity of places and experiences.

Salman Rushdie

The question of representing India in literature is central to the work of Salman Rushdie. Born a Bombay Muslim in 1947 (the year of independence and partition), his family migrated to Pakistan, from where Rushdie was sent to school in England, completing his education at Cambridge. His work is closely bound up with the politics, history and culture of the Indian subcontinent. However, as has been seen (page 13, above), it is written from the perspective of exile, and this fact has affected both the style of his work and his relationship to the region he is writing about.

As a migrant Rushdie has encountered both the need to recreate the past and the uncertainty which comes with rootlessness. The narrator of his novel *Shame* (1983), which satirises the politics of Pakistan, addresses the reader directly on this issue. In the passage below, he compares the plight of the individual migrant to a newly created country, referring here to both Pakistan and Bangladesh (formerly East Pakistan which broke away from the Western part in 1971):

> When individuals come unstuck from their native land, they are called migrants. When nations do the same thing (Bangladesh), the act is called secession. What is the best thing about migrant peoples and seceded nations? I think it is their hopefulness ... And what's the worst thing? It is the emptiness of one's luggage. I'm speaking of invisible suitcases, not the physical, perhaps cardboard, variety containing a few meaning drained mementoes. We have come unstuck from more than land. We have floated upwards from history, from memory, from Time.
>
> I may be such a person. Pakistan may be such a country ...
>
> To build Pakistan it was necessary to cover up Indian history, to deny that Indian centuries lay just beneath the surface of Pakistani Standard Time. The past was rewritten; there was nothing else to be done.

▶ What different senses of the past are presented in this passage? How might the passage be seen to reflect an awareness of both personal and national fictions?

Issues of narration and representation are at the centre of Rushdie's writing. In both *Midnight's Children* (1981) and *Shame*, the narrator addresses the reader directly about the process of narration. Rushdie rarely allows his reader simply to suspend disbelief. The overtly fictional, stylised nature of his writing is emphasised, encouraging the reader to regard what is presented with healthy distrust.

This departure from a conventionally realist style is a key aspect of Rushdie's work, which is often described as **'magic realist'.** This label conveys Rushdie's use of supernatural or fantastical occurrences as an essential part of his fictional world. At one point, for instance, Saleem Sinai, the narrator of *Midnight's Children,* becomes transformed into a sniffer dog used in the Bangladeshi war of independence. All of midnight's children, those born at the time of India's independence, possess special powers; Saleem, born on the stroke of midnight, 15 August 1947, has the telepathic ability to pick up signals from around India:

> I should explain that as my mental faculty increased, I found that it was possible not only to pick up the children's transmissions; not only to broadcast my own messages; but also (since I seem to be stuck with this radio metaphor) to act as a sort of national network, so that by opening my transformed mind to all the children I could turn it into a kind of forum in which they could talk to each other. So, in the early days of 1958, the five hundred and eighty one children would assemble, for one hour, between midnight and one a.m., in the lok sabha or parliament of my brain.

The magic realist author is not limited by the same restrictions or laws that govern everyday reality and is therefore able to explore the world fully through his imagination. In *Midnight's Children* this allows Rushdie to create a fictional world through which to comment on the political realities of modern India. It is a world full of symbols which the reader can then interpret. For instance, the fate of Saleem, who begins to write his story before his body falls apart because it has been 'buffeted by too much history' and is 'slowly disintegrating', can be said to represent the fate of India itself; after all, the moment of Saleem's auspicious birth meant that he was 'handcuffed to history'.

Another characteristic of Rushdie's magic realism is the use of Indian mythology. Saleem, with his long nose and large ears, can be seen as the figure of Ganesha (the Hindu god of literature, known for his gentle nature). In the novel, he is contrasted with 'Shiva of the knees', born at the same time as Saleem, but representing violence and destruction in India (in Hindu mythology, the god Shiva is often seen as the destroyer). Rushdie appropriates these traditional myths, as a means of representing conflicting forces in Indian history:

Shiva and Saleem, victor and victim; understand our rivalry, and you
will gain an understanding of the age in which you live. (The reverse
of this statement is also true.)

However, the eclectic, inventive and wide-ranging style of *Midnight's Children* is
influenced by genres as diverse as modern cinema and oral storytelling, by various
Western and Eastern artistic forms. Furthermore, Rushdie's work challenges the
usefulness of such pure definitions as Eastern or Western; Shiva, for instance,
speaks with American slang.

This **hybridity** is an essential part of Rushdie's work and has a particular
significance within an Indian context. Given the increasing influence of religious
fundamentalism in India and Pakistan, with its emphasis on tradition and cultural
purity, Rushdie's ability to cross cultural and imaginative boundaries (for example,
the Muslim Saleem draws on Hindu mythology) can be read as a way of
emphasising the pluralistic nature of Indian society.

Anita Desai

Born in Delhi in 1937 to an Indian father and German mother, Desai has lived the
majority of her life in India. Like Narayan's, her work is primarily concerned with
the individual psychology of her characters. In an interview with Feroza Jusswalla,
she has emphasised this aspect:

If they were simply representatives, they would be like cardboard
creatures, they would be posters rather than paintings. They would
simply stand for a certain society or a certain moment in history,
which of course they don't.

The emphasis on 'paintings' as opposed to 'posters' reflects the depth and texture
of her portraits, which often explore the inner worlds of her characters. Consider
the following lines from her novel, *Clear Light Of Day* (1980), set in Delhi. The
passage follows a description of the cremation of Aunt Mira, at which Bim and Raja,
brother and sister, were present:

Yet for a long time Bim continued to see her, was certain that she saw
her: the shrunken little body naked, trailing a torn shred of a nightie,
a wisp of pubic hair, as she slipped surreptitiously along the hedge,
head bent low as if she hoped no one would notice her as she hurried
towards the well. Bim would catch her breath and shut her eyes
before opening them again to stare wildly at the hedge and find only

the tassles of the malaviscus dangling there, like leering red tongues, and nothing else.

Clear Light of Day is very much concerned with family memories and experiences. However, it also conveys the cultural and historical world which shapes those experiences. The splitting up of the family reflects the break up of India because of partition. *Clear Light of Day* can be seen as Desai's response to the turbulence of independence and the loss generated during that period.

Part of Desai's significance lies in her ability to convey the experience and generally restricted position of women in Indian society. Consider the following passage from her novel *In Custody* (1984). It is narrated from the perspective of Deven, the main character. Interestingly, Desai has said that she chose to write the novel from a male perspective because it was 'the only way I could step out into the world and write about wider concerns and experiences ... Women are still chiefly confined to family and domesticity':

> She looked up as he came in. She had wrapped the end of her sari around her mouth to keep out the dust as she swept. She pulled it off with one finger, letting it fall, and stared at him. 'So, still spending your time in Delhi?' she asked heavily.
>
> He stood very still, although he was immensely agitated, and immensely worn out by a sleepless night spent at a bus depot. 'Why didn't you tell me you were returning today? I would have come to the station to meet you.'
>
> 'I did write,' she snapped, and pointed to an unopened letter that lay on the small table next to his chair. 'You never opened it,' she accused him, and started sweeping again.
>
> He did not move out of her way but stood watching her crawl about the floor, sweeping the dust into little hills before her ... He considered touching her, putting an arm around her stooped shoulder and drawing her to him. How else could he tell her he shared all her disappointment and woe?
>
> But he could not make that move: it would have permanently undermined his position of power over her, a position that was as important to her as to him: if she ceased to believe in it, what would there be for her to do, where would she go?

▶ What might the passage suggest about the Indian male perception of women? How would you describe the relationship between husband and wife? How do you respond to the character of his wife, Sarla?

In Custody has been described as Anita Desai's most public and political work. On one level, the novel is about the place of the minority language Urdu (the main language of India's Muslims and the official language of Pakistan) in a state increasingly dominated by Hindi (a major language of Hindus) after independence.

▶ Read the extract from *In Custody* (Part 3, pages 77–78). Deven, a teacher of Hindi, has introduced himself to a famous Urdu poet, Nur, because he wishes to interview him.

How might the passage seem to reflect cultural tensions in India? To what extent might Deven be seen as representing the need for tolerance across Indian culture? How do you respond to the character of Nur? To what extent does he seem individual and to what extent is he representative of a group of people? A whole culture even?

Arundhati Roy

As with Desai, Arundhati Roy's work shows real psychological depth while conveying the realities of culture and history. *The God of Small Things* (1997) is set in the state of Kerala and reflects the political climate of the area, where the Communist Party is particularly strong.

The novel examines the effects of hierarchies within both family and state, the rules which govern human behaviour and the fate of those who break such rules. Much of the book is written from the point of view of two twins, Rahel and Estha, and is a disturbing tale of the destruction of their innocence. In the lines below, an older Rahel reflects on the nature of 'the laws' and upon breaking 'the rules'. Ammu is her mother:

> Perhaps, Ammu, Estha and she were the worst transgressors. But it wasn't just them. It was others too. They all broke the rules. They all crossed into forbidden territory. They all tampered with the laws that lay down who should be loved and how. And how much. The laws that make grandmothers grandmothers, uncles uncles, mothers mothers cousins cousins, jam jam and jelly jelly.
>
> It was a time when uncles became fathers, mothers lovers, and cousins died and had funerals.
>
> It was a time when the unthinkable became thinkable and the impossible really happened.

Such laws affect not only relationships within the family, but the position of women in society, the treatment of untouchables (even though the Indian constitution outlaws discrimination on grounds of caste) and the experience of children, who are often victims at the hands of adults.

Within the novel, different forms of oppression and abuse become linked through the lives of the characters. The *God of Small Things* can be seen as presenting the fate of those who do not fit within traditional boundaries. As the work of Anand and Rao had done before independence, the novel itself crosses boundaries. This is done not only through its protest at the position of women or untouchables, but in broaching taboo subjects, such as sexual abuse and incest. It is also achieved through Roy's highly individual, inventive style; like Rushdie, she experiments with language and narrative structure in order to shock, challenge and move the reader. The world she presents is also a hybrid one: Chacko, the twins' uncle, is an Anglophile from a Syrian Christian family who pretends to have **Marxist** affiliations; the Communist, Comrade Pillai, who politically disagrees with discrimination, refuses to help Velutha partly because of his caste. However, if Rushdie's *Midnight's Children* is the narrative of a country, Roy's work focuses on the minute and the specific, the 'small things', the tragedies surrounding a family in a specific part of India.

Africa

The historical and cultural context

Though the word 'Africa' seems to imply one place and one people, in reality the continent is made up of over 800 different ethnic groups, each with their own language, culture and history. The boundaries of modern African states, created by European colonialists, are just one, very recent, layer of African identity.

When discussing the impact of British colonialism in Africa, it is important to bear in mind that it took different forms in different parts of Africa. Also, Africans themselves responded to it in very different ways.

This point can be illustrated by looking at British involvement in two different areas of what is now modern Nigeria. Because of a policy of 'indirect rule' (rule through minimal political and cultural interference), the British impact in the Muslim-dominated Northern Territory was limited: taxes were extracted using already existing hierarchies. However, where there were no previously existing hierarchies, as in the Ibo East, the British imposed a system of 'warrant chiefs', which was at odds with traditional, community-based political structures. The impact of this, combined with zealous missionary activity in the region, was immense: not only were 'warrant chiefs' the puppets of the colonial administration, but the essential structure and values of Ibo life were undermined. It is hardly surprising that there were many more conflicts in the East than in the North.

The Scramble for Africa

Historically, the trade for slaves and gold along the west coast of Africa was conducted by African middlemen at the coast. No significant British incursions were made into the continent until the 19th century, yet by 1900 only Ethiopia and Liberia were not under European control.

The Scramble for Africa was a race between rival European powers in the 1880s to take as much of Africa as possible. At the Berlin Conference of 1885, the European powers divided the continent amongst themselves. Despite often fierce and prolonged resistance, such as from the Ashanti in modern Ghana, the Zulu in South Africa or the Matabele in Zimbabwe, European technological superiority, particularly in the area of weapons, meant that eventual domination was inevitable.

First, economic factors behind empire need to be kept in mind. Manchester merchants sought to secure cheaper prices when buying cotton and palm oil from the Niger Delta in West Africa. Nigeria was to become both a major source of raw materials and a market for goods manufactured in Britain. The discovery of gold in 1886 at Witwatersrand in South Africa, as well as diamonds at Kimberley, created a massive influx of British investment into South Africa. Such economic motivations help to explain the use of both forced and cheap labour in British Africa. To entrepreneurs and settlers, black labour was another commodity to be acquired as cheaply as possible. In West Africa, forced labour for road building became a potent symbol of British rule.

European attitudes towards Africa

Psychological factors are equally relevant when approaching post-colonial writing. These helped to create the culture which shaped empire and, because they informed colonial behaviour on the ground, the experience of Africans themselves. African writers would, in very different ways, have to address these key areas.

A sense of racial superiority on the part of whites was a legacy of the slave trade, but the growth of popular, biological theories of evolution played a large part in strengthening such attitudes. Darwin's *On the Origin of Species* (1859) greatly influenced thinking about race: Africans were perceived as living primitively in a state of evolutionary underdevelopment. In depictions of Africa, the cities of Benin or the Ashanti kingdom were edited out; 'civilisation' on either coast was seen as the product of Arab influence; it was, and by some still is, believed that the ruins of Great Zimbabwe could not have been built by Africans. Europeans increasingly saw Africa as an image of their own pre-historic past. Sir Samuel Baker, the explorer, speaking to an audience in 1874, said that as Central Africa was

> … without a history … we must therefore conclude that the races of man which now inhabit [this region] are unchanged from the

prehistoric tribes who were the original inhabitants.
(cited in M. E. Chamberlain *The Scramble for Africa,* 1974)

▶ Significantly, Baker's perception was not an isolated one. Read the passage from Joseph Conrad's (1857–1924) novella 'Heart of Darkness'(1902) (Part 3, pages 70–71). What similarities can you see between the ideas and attitudes expressed in that work and those outlined above?

Missionaries in Africa

The impact of missionaries is particularly controversial: opinions are divided about the damage and benefits that missionary activity brought. There is no doubt, however, that missions in Africa were a powerful force which radically altered African society.

Groups such as The United Society for the Propagation of the Gospel and The Church Missionary Society genuinely believed that they belonged to a superior culture whose hallmarks were literacy, European manners and values, and technological progress. They generally had little or no knowledge of the cultures that they were trying to convert. Often disgusted by practices of polygamy, witchcraft and superstition (as they saw it), the missionaries desired to 'save' and 'redeem' Africans.

Essentially, the issue was not simply religious, but also political and cultural. It was clear to many Africans that the Christian churches were often the allies of empire. In Kenya, where missionary activity was particularly intense, a saying of the Kikuyu (the country's largest ethnic group) proclaimed that there was no difference between a missionary and a settler.

Furthermore, mission schools provided a cheap administrative workforce of clerks for the lower ranks of colonial administration. Importantly, converts were told to pay their taxes ('Render unto Caesar the things which are Caesar's'), place their faith in God and be humble and obedient. On one level, missions were part of the process of denigrating traditional African culture. They were opposed to many of the indigenous customs and hierarchies which bound communities together. The impact of missionary activity would therefore be a key issue for modern African writers.

Another purpose of mission education was the creation of a Christian, African élite. Though higher education was very limited, an English speaking élite was created, most notably in Freetown, Sierra Leone, at Fourah Bay College (established 1827). Graduates entered the respectable professions of law, medicine, teaching and the church, and initially sought to distinguish themselves from traditional African culture, to the extent that they later became nicknamed the 'Black Victorians'.

One impact of missions was to divide African societies, promoting European superiority and seeking to eradicate traditional practices and beliefs. However, mission education was a double-edged sword. Many African writers in English have been educated at élite mission schools, as have prominent nationalist politicians.

Modern African writing in English

Modern African writing in English counteracts the negative **stereotypes** of the colonial period. African writers have had to dismantle powerful myths about African inferiority and assert their distinctive African cultures. In the post-independence period, the role of the writer has become more explicitly political, whether under the regime of apartheid in South Africa or criticising government corruption in Kenya, to name but two examples. More than in any other region, African writers have been imprisoned or had their work banned for speaking out against oppressive regimes.

The three most prominent African writers since the 1950s are Chinua Achebe and Wole Soyinka from Nigeria and Ngugi wa Thiong'o from Kenya. Each has responded in different ways to the problems facing African writers in English. These include: the use of English, the representation of Africans and their history, post-independence political corruption and the significance of traditional culture in modern Africa.

Though these writers were the first to gain international recognition, they were not the first Africans writing in English. As early as 1881, Edward Blyden, as President of Liberia College, used English as a means of asserting African identity, proclaiming:

> The African must advance by methods of his own. He must possess a
> power distinct from that of the European ... We must show that we
> are able to go alone, to carve out our own way.

Later, in Nigeria, Cyprian Ekwensi published *Ikolo the Wrestler and other Igbo Tales* (1947), a collection of oral folk tales. In the 1950s, Amos Tutuola published *The Palm-Wine Drinkard* (1952) and *In the Bush of Ghosts* (1954), in which he used dialect to draw upon Yoruba (of the Yoruba ethnic group from Western Nigeria) folk tales and mythology. Achebe, Soyinka and Ngugi belong to a developing tradition of African writing in English, and have themselves influenced a new generation of African writers, such as the Zimbabwean Tsitsi Dangarembga, author of *Nervous Conditions* (1988), and the Nigerian Ben Okri, author of *The Famished Road* (1991). (There are extracts from both these novels in Part 3, pages 84–85, and pages 86–87.) Their significance lies in the fact that their work not only broke new ground artistically, but also enabled others to develop their own style and perspective.

Chinua Achebe

Born in 1930 in Ogidi, Eastern Nigeria, to Christian parents, Chinua Achebe was the first black African writer in English to gain widespread critical acclaim from the international English-speaking world. His first novel, *Things Fall Apart* (1958) is regarded as a milestone of African literature. It became the first novel by an African to be studied in African secondary schools; the appearance of a paperback edition made it an affordable best-seller in Nigeria, selling 20,000 copies there in 1964.

Achebe's essays about the role of the writer in Africa, his autobiographical reflections on colonialism and independence, and his writing about Ibo culture (the ethnic group to which he belongs) provide insights which are particularly useful when approaching post-colonial African literature (see Part 5, page 121 for details).

In the following lines from his essay, 'The Novelist as Teacher' (1965), Achebe discusses the role of the writer within African society:

> Here then is an adequate revolution for me to espouse – to help my society regain belief in itself and put away the complexes of years of denigration and self-abasement ...
> The writer cannot expect to be excused from the task of re-education and regeneration that must be done. In fact he should march right in front. For he is after all – as Ezekiel Mphalele says in his 'African Image' – the sensitive point of his community.

The essay was written only four years after Nigeria gained independence. Note how Achebe defines his role as a writer in terms of what he can achieve for his society ('to help my society regain belief in itself') and how this is entwined with redressing the negative psychological effects of colonialism in Africa ('complexes of years of denigration and self-abasement'). The writer is not an isolated figure, but 'the sensitive point of his community'.

Many post-colonial writers perceive themselves as serving the needs of the societies to which they belong (in this case the development of Nigerian pride and nationalism); therefore, such writing has a social, as well as artistic, function. As such, post-colonial texts can be seen as vehicles for a broader historical and cultural process, that of redressing the negative effects of colonialism; in other words, being part of the process of 're-education and regeneration'.

Things Fall Apart is predominantly set in Umuofia, an Ibo village in Eastern Nigeria, when the white man first arrives. It is as much concerned with a full presentation of the Ibo way of life, as with the main character, Okonkwo. The latter part of the novel presents the impact of missionaries and the colonial administration upon Ibo society.

▶ Read the extract from *Things Fall Apart* (Part 3, pages 78–79) taken from early in the novel, and consider how it reflects Achebe's aims as a writer.

Throughout the novel, Achebe uses original Ibo vocabulary and a style of English sensitive to the rhythms and pace of that language; he draws on proverbs, folk tales and techniques developed by oral storytellers.

▶ In his essay, 'The African Writer and the English Language' (1964), Achebe wrote that the African writer should 'aim at fashioning out an English which is at once universal and able to carry his peculiar experience ... a new English, ... altered to suit its new African surroundings'. What does this statement suggest about Achebe's attitude to the use of English?

Things Fall Apart presents a view of pre-colonial Ibo society which is part of Achebe's attempt to reclaim African history from an African perspective. The phrase 're-education and regeneration' carries with it very real implications for how Africans, particularly school children, should learn about Africa. Within the context of a newly independent Nigeria, Achebe's historical novels can be seen as voicing the experience of Africans denied by European accounts.

However, his work is far from romantic or propagandist. His third novel, *Arrow of God* (1964), set when the British were establishing 'indirect rule' in Eastern Nigeria, is concerned with how Africans themselves responded to colonialism. They are not depicted as passive victims but as active agents in their own history. Furthermore, the novel focuses on internal Ibo politics and personal rivalries, particularly regarding the position of Ezeulu, the Chief Priest of Umuaro.

In Achebe's second novel, *No Longer At Ease* (1960), he deals primarily with the experiences of a 'been to' character (one who has been educated or lived in England), Obi, and his return to Nigeria in the period immediately preceding independence. Much of the novel is concerned with the conflicting loyalties and aspirations within the mind of this modern Nigerian. Through this, a realistic portrait of contemporary life in Lagos is built up.

The climax of this conflict is Obi's desire to marry an *osu*, a girl from an outcast family, a concept which his own family and wider clan cannot understand. The breaking of the engagement by Clara and her subsequent abortion, combined with Obi's trial for accepting bribes, paint a bleak picture, both for the individual characters and the nation. The novel establishes the theme of corruption in modern African fiction, and seeks to examine the causes of this.

Achebe's presentation of Obi's predicament emphasises the complexity of modern Nigeria. As with *A Man of the People* (1966), Achebe explores the hybridity (mixed nature) of the country, both in terms of the disparate groups within the state and the conflicting influences acting on the mind of the main character. Significantly, Nigeria itself is a federation of originally separate groups. The country is divided into three main regions (the predominantly Muslim North, the Ibo East and Yoruba West), with over 200 different language communities within the modern state. As a reflection of this diversity, the vocabulary of *A Man of the People* contains words from Ibo, Hausa and Yoruba, as well as pidgin (a dialect of English).

As a satire of post-independence politics and corruption, *A Man of the People* presents us with a national and political realm that is a moral vacuum, in which individuals such as Chief Nanga are driven only by personal ambition. Achebe undoubtedly based the novel on his observations of independent Nigeria. The novel's ending, that of a military coup, is particularly poignant given Nigeria's political history. In 1966, two years after the novel was completed, Major-General Aguiyi-Ironsi established military dictatorship after a predominantly Ibo group of army officers staged a successful coup.

However, the work's relevance is not purely Nigerian. As the anonymity of the country suggests, corruption, political intimidation and the adoption of the privileges and trappings of colonialism by a political élite have become a common feature of post-independence Africa.

Wole Soyinka

Soyinka's writing, which gained him the Nobel Prize for Literature in 1986, encompasses the areas of drama, poetry, novels, memoirs, essays and lectures. Soyinka himself has refused to be neatly categorised, either artistically or politically. He has always sought to distance himself from trends, proclaiming famously about **Negritude**, 'The tiger does not pronounce its tigritude. It pounces.' (Makere, 1962) Negritude was a literary movement, first started by Aimé Cesaire and Leopold Senghor, which sought to glorify, even idealise, traditional African culture and experience. It was particularly prominent in French colonies such as Senegal, of which Senghor became President in 1960, but it also influenced a wider spectrum of black writers. Soyinka's statement shows how as a thinker and writer, he rejects simple solutions or manifestos.

Like Achebe, Soyinka was born into a family of the educated Nigerian élite and was educated at Government College and Ibadan University. He broadened his English studies at Leeds University and became a play-reader at the Royal Court Theatre, London. On returning to Nigeria, he threw himself into Nigerian cultural life, forming the Masks Theatre Company, based at the University of Ibadan, in order to perform new African drama.

Despite a range of European influences on his work, from Samuel Beckett's absurdist *Waiting for Godot* (1955), which presents human life as without purpose or coherence, to earlier 17th-century comedy of manners (drama which seeks to ridicule social behaviour), Soyinka is very much an African dramatist. In his drama, he incorporates many elements of religious ritual and folk theatre, including pageants, mime, dance and the use of masks (see pages 62–63).

Indeed, Soyinka has developed a theory of drama which draws upon Yoruba religion and traditional drama. Much of this is based on a belief in 'The Fourth Stage', a twilight world between the living, the dead and the unborn, where transition occurs, and is full of possibilities for creation and destruction. For Soyinka, plays are a means by which the struggles between positive and negative forces can be acted out. One could say that modern Nigeria, still in the process of being born, is itself a place of flux and of competing forces, whether those of artistic expression or political oppression, and that Soyinka's drama reflects this.

One prominent example of this type of drama is *A Dance of the Forests* (1960). The play was first performed as part of the Nigerian Independence Celebrations (though excluded from the official programme) in October 1960. Through it, Soyinka explores fundamental spiritual and historical issues, such as modern Nigeria's relationship to its ancestors, to the environment and to the realm of gods and spirits. Set predominantly in the Forest, a potentially dangerous meeting place between the human and the spiritual, the living and the dead, the play is populated with both human Town Dwellers and mythological Forest Dwellers, such as Ogun the patron god of carvers and metalworkers.

In the following extract, Forest Head, a leading deity, uses a Questioner to receive the Dead Woman before the Spirits of the Forest dance for her and the Dead Man:

[First, there is total stillness, emphasised by the sound of moisture dripping to the ground. Forest Head is sitting on a large stone, statuesque, the Questioner stands beside him ... The Dead Woman enters, dead as on first appearance. She behaves exactly as before, hesitant, seemingly lost.]

QUESTIONER Who sent you?
DEAD WOMAN I am certain she had no womb, but I think
            It was a woman.
QUESTIONER Before your time?
            Was it before your time?
DEAD WOMAN I have come to ask that of
            The knowing ones. My knowledge is
            The hate alone. The little ball of hate
            Alone consumed me. Wet runnels

```
                      Of the earth brought me hither.
                      Call Forest Head. Say someone comes
                      For all the rest. Say someone asks –
                      Was it for this, for this,
                      Children plagued their mothers?
      QUESTIONER      A mother, and in haste?
                      Were there no men? No barren women,
                      Aged and toothless women?
                      What called you forth beyond the backyard fence?
                      Beyond the cooking pots? What made you deaf
                      To the life that begged within you?
                      Had he no claim?
      DEAD WOMAN      For him. It was for him.
      QUESTIONER      You should have lived for him. Did you dare
                      Snatch death from those that gasped for breath? ...
                      [The woman is silent]
      FOREST HEAD     Every day. Every hour. Where will it end?
                      Child, there is no choice but one of suffering
                      And those who tread the understreams
                      Add ashes to the hairs
                      Of Forest Father. Rest awhile.
                      The beings of the Forest have been called
                      To dance the welcome, to quiet your spirit
                      Torn losely by the suddenness. And roots
                      Have brought us news of another son
                      And he has come a longer way, almost
                      They murmur, from quite another world.
```

▶ How do you feel a sense of 'The Fourth Stage' is developed in the above extract?

A sense of change can be seen in Soyinka's light satire on modern Nigeria, *The Lion and the Jewel* (1959). In the following scene, Lakunle, the mission-educated school teacher full of modern ideas, tries to woo Sidi, the village beauty. Sidi teasingly begins by responding to the fact that Lakunle does not wish to pay the traditional bride-price (a payment to the bride's father):

```
      SIDI            They will say I was no virgin
                      That I was forced to sell my shame
                      And marry you without a price.
      LAKUNLE         A savage custom, barbaric, outdated,
                      Rejected, denounced, accursed, degrading,
                      Humiliating, unspeakable, redundant.
                      Retrogressive, remarkable, unpalatable.
```

SIDI	Is the bag empty? Why did you stop?
LAKUNLE	I own only the Shorter Companion
	Dictionary, but I have ordered
	The Longer One – you wait!
SIDI	Just pay the price.
LAKUNLE	*[with a sudden shout]*
	An ignoble custom, infamous, ignominious
	Shaming our heritage before the world.
	Sidi, I do not seek a wife
	To fetch and carry,
	To cook and scrub,
	To bring forth children by the gross …
SIDI	Heaven forgive you! Do you now scorn
	Child-bearing in a wife?

It is one of Soyinka's characteristics as a dramatist to satirise all sections of society; later in the play both Sidi, and the lecherous Baroka, the Bale (chief) of the village, are ridiculed.

As the political situation in Nigeria deteriorated, Soyinka's satire became more political and the humour darker. Soyinka's increasing despair at Nigerian politics is reflected in *Madmen and Specialists* (1970). (There is an extract from the play in Part 3, pages 81–83.) The play is a direct response to the Biafran war (1967–1970), during which Soyinka was imprisoned for two years while on a peace mission to Northern Nigeria. The play deals with torture and the senselessness of the atrocities committed, and is written in a bleak style reminiscent of Beckett's *Waiting for Godot*.

As with other African writers, Soyinka has spent much of his life in exile because of political persecution in his homeland.

Ngugi wa Thiong'o

Ngugi wa Thiong'o is perhaps East Africa's most politically committed writer. Born near Nairobi, Kenya, in 1938, the son of an *ahoi* (a dispossessed peasant farmer), Ngugi has always had a concern for the poor and for social justice at the heart of his work. His writing is intimately involved with Kenyan history and politics. Ngugi has himself written:

The poet and the politician have certainly many things in common.
Both trade in words. Both are created by the same reality of the
world around us … Literature and politics are about living men, actual
men and women and children, breathing, eating, crying, laughing,

creating, dying, growing, men in history of which they are its products and its makers.

(Writers in Politics, 1975)

Politics for Ngugi is reflected in the daily lives of 'actual' people. Like the Caribbean writer, C.L.R. James (see page 52), Ngugi has become increasingly influenced by Marxist thinking. His novels have become as concerned with analysing political and economic structures as with the individual psychology and experiences of characters.

Ngugi shares similar concerns to Achebe and Soyinka, such as depicting traditional African customs authentically, analysing the impact of colonialism and the nature of post-independence society. His writing, however, reflects the specific experiences of Kenyans, and, in particular, the Kikuyu tribe to which he belongs. The experience of colonisation in Kenya was different from that in Nigeria because of the amount of land which was taken by white settlers. Native peoples were moved to infertile reserves and thus forced to work on white-owned estates in order to survive. Furthermore, missionary activity was particularly vehement in Kenya. In contrast to the expectation of black majority rule in Nigeria, the white settler population in Kenya was particularly oppressive against nationalist politicians: the Mau Mau war of independence was among the bloodiest and dirtiest that the British fought in Africa. The divisions within Kikuyu society, which came to the fore and were utilised by the British, still divide Kenya today.

A Grain Of Wheat (1967) is set in the days leading up to *Uhuru,* Kenyan independence. The characters, black and white, reflect on how their lives were affected by Mau Mau. Through a complex series of 'flashbacks', a realistic sense of individual histories is created at this moment of national significance. Ngugi gradually reveals the deep psychological wounds within ordinary Kenyans caused by the conflict, and the pessimistic prospects for the future. The novel is as much about guilt and betrayal as about courage. Ngugi explores the motivations behind such betrayal, whether caused by personal predicament or the colonial system, and the complex allegiances and deceptions that took place during Mau Mau.

Crucially, however, the novel presents the stories of those involved in Mau Mau from their own perspective. To many in the West, Mau Mau came to represent the white man's worst fears about African 'savagery', despite the fact that only 95 Europeans were killed, as opposed to 11,503 ordinary Kikuyu. Only recently has the full extent of colonial brutality been calculated.

▶ Read the extract from *A Grain of Wheat* (Part 3, pages 80–81) in which a detention camp that held Mau Mau suspects is depicted. Consider what purpose such writing might have, both inside and outside Kenya.

In *Petals of Blood* (1977), set in independent Kenya, Ngugi examines the workings of a society built on the suffering of the majority. The novel is critical of the 'neo-colonial' African élite, those Africans who have taken the positions once held by Europeans, adopted European values and done nothing to help the plight of the ordinary African, despite supporting foreign international companies.

He contrasts the opulence of the estates owned by the élite with the poverty of the shanty towns. Again, Ngugi examines the betrayal of Africans by Africans; how this leads to further exploitation and oppression and how it denies people the freedoms they hoped for after independence.

Shortly after the novel's publication, Ngugi was arrested and detained without trial. In prison he began to write prose in Gikuyu, rejecting the international medium of English. This can be seen as a symbolic act. In choosing to write in Gikuyu, Ngugi was identifying himself with the peasants whose causes he represented and rejecting the language of the coloniser, which is also the language of the élite. For Ngugi, language is as political as anything else. Rejecting English was part of counteracting the damaging effects of colonialism and the dependency on European culture.

South Africa: the historical and cultural context

Apartheid, which means 'separateness' in Afrikaans, the language developed by the original Dutch settlers, was the system of racial control inherited from the British and formally established by the Afrikaner National Party after it won the 1948 election. The basis of the system was a racist set of beliefs which held that Asians, coloureds and blacks were inferior to whites. In practice, this meant that the lives of the coloured/black population could be exploited to maintain the economic superiority of the whites, who never numbered more than 20% of the population. It was made possible by the introduction of the Population Registration Act in 1950; the Pass Law meant that it was compulsory to carry a 'pass' which identified the racial group of each holder. The use of passes meant that the government could control the population movement of blacks so that all white suburbs could be 'protected' and blacks in search of work could be 'directed' to wherever their labour was needed. The early 1950s also saw the Suppression of Communism Act; effectively this outlawed any opposition to apartheid, as communism was so broadly defined that it included any opposition activity outside parliament, inside which blacks had no say.

Gradually, apartheid came to influence every aspect of life in South Africa, from the use of lavatories and buses to restaurants and universities. Under the Immorality Act, sexual relationships and marriage between the races were banned. Blacks were treated as unwanted aliens in their own country. One culmination of racial oppression was the Sharpeville massacre in March 1960, when police opened fire on demonstrators opposed to the Pass Laws. Sixty nine people were killed and over a hundred injured. In response to further protests by organisations such as the African National Congress, the regime became increasingly oppressive.

The 1970s saw the rise of the Black Consciousness Movement. Initially it was student based, and grew out of the South African Students Organisation (established 1968), which was formed by black students who felt that their views could no longer be represented within the liberal, but white-dominated National Union of South African Students. At its heart was the belief that blacks had to become conscious of their own identity as a route towards political power. The activists of the 1970s were becoming increasingly radical. Steve Biko, who was to die of a brain haemorrhage while being detained without charge, was its principal voice.

Tensions reached a peak when pupils in Soweto schools revolted against the decree that Afrikaans should be the language of instruction. On 16 June, 1976, black youths boycotted schools and took to the streets to demonstrate. Though the protest was peaceful, the police attacked crowds, killing an unarmed 13-year-old, Hector Peterson. This sparked off unrest in which 575 people were killed by the following February. Increasingly, the government came to rely upon armed police to control the country.

Despite the realisation of black majority rule across the rest of Africa, South Africa, which had become an independent 'dominion' in 1910, and left the Commonwealth in 1961, was governed by a regime whose characteristics extended and systematised the worst aspects of white colonial domination. Apartheid formally ended when Nelson Mandela, who had been imprisoned from 1964 to 1990, became the first black President of South Africa in 1994, under South Africa's fully democratic constitution.

South African literature and apartheid

The playwright Athol Fugard and the novelists Nadine Gordimer and J.M. Coetzee are the three South African writers who have gained the greatest reputations abroad, even if their works were condemned and, at times, banned within South Africa itself. All three writers remained in South Africa at a period when other artists and intellectuals chose to observe the increasingly confrontational situation from adopted countries. The nature of life in an increasingly violent and repressive country is at the heart of their work, as is the problematic position of the white writer in such a situation. The issue of boundaries between races and the divergent perspectives they create is central to their writing.

Athol Fugard

Drama, such as the performance theatre of Athol Fugard, played an important part in speaking out against apartheid. Fugard sought to involve black actors in the writing and directing process as a means of **empowerment**. Most notably, his work with the Serpent Players of the New Brighton township sought to release the creative potential of the actors, whose improvisations were based on their personal experiences under apartheid. Such mutual collaboration led to striking plays, such as *The Coat* (1966), *Sizwe Bansi is Dead* (1972) and *The Island* (1973). Fugard sought to 'shatter white complacency and its conspiracy of silence' (from Fugard's *Notebooks,* quoted in the introduction to *Township Plays,* 1993).

▶ Read the extract taken from the opening of *The Coat* (Part 3, pages 88–89). How might the opening of this play have challenged the expectations of white theatre-goers? What do you learn about the intentions of the Serpent Players from the extract?

Nadine Gordimer

Nadine Gordimer won the Nobel Prize for Literature in 1991 for her treatment of race relations within her country. She has said that all her work takes its power from the nature of life in South Africa.

The following extract is from an early short story, 'Six Feet of the Country' (1956), which is set on a farm outside Johannesburg. The narrator is a white male who considers himself to be a 'liberal', meaning non-racist in this context.

> Albert did not answer; he had given me the path, and was walking along beside me in the tall dead grass. When the light of the torch caught his face, I saw that he looked acutely embarrassed. 'What's this all about?' I said. He lowered his head under the glance of the light. 'It's not me, baas. I don't know. Petrus he send me.'
>
> Irritated I hurried him along to the huts. And there, on Petrus's iron bedstead, with its brick stilts, was a young man, dead. On his forehead there was a light, cold sweat; his body was warm. The boys stood around as they do in the kitchen when it is discovered that someone has broken a dish – uncooperative, silent. Somebody's wife hung about in the shadows, her hands wrung together under her apron.
>
> I had not seen a dead man since the war. This was very different. I felt like the others – extraneous, useless …
>
> I turned to Petrus. 'Who was this boy? What was he doing here?' The light of a candle on the floor showed that Petrus was weeping. He followed me out the door.
>
> When we were outside, in the dark, I waited for him to speak. But

he didn't. 'Now, come on, Petrus, you must tell me who this boy was. Was he a friend of yours?'

'He's my brother, baas. He came from Rhodesia to look for work.'

▶ How would you describe the relationship between black and white in this passage? What is revealed by the way the narrator and the blacks address each other?

The fact that Gordimer has chosen to write from the perspective of a white liberal, as opposed to an Afrikaner nationalist, may be significant. Perhaps the passage reveals how the white liberal, for all his caring intentions, is still very much the master, the 'baas'. Throughout the story, the white liberal narrator betrays himself, his values and prejudices, to the reader.

The passage has another obvious but important function: to convey the effects of apartheid to the international community. The fact that South African writers often have a dual audience, both inside and outside the country, is an important aspect to bear in mind when approaching their writing.

During the 1970s Gordimer began openly to support the armed struggle of the African National Congress (Nelson Mandela had been commander-in-chief of military operations), and became increasingly aware of the conflicting cultural and political pressures between Afrikaner nationalism, black consciousness and white liberalism. As the above passage suggests, Gordimer was critical of liberals because, though they might have disagreed with apartheid, few were prepared actually to lose the privileges created by the system.

Gordimer's political commitment showed itself through an increasing need to include the black voice within her work. This can be seen in the novel, *Burger's Daughter* (1979). The central character, Rosemarie Burger, is the daughter of a white communist, who spends much of the novel attempting to escape the political expectations put upon her. In the passage below, she has been taken to a party of black activists in the township (designated black living area) of Soweto. Much of the dialogue has been a debate about the extent to which blacks and whites can co-operate in the struggle to overthrow apartheid. The speaker is a black activist:

We are educating the black to know he is strong and be proud of it. We are going to get rid of the capitalist and racist system but not as a 'working class'. That's a white nonsense, here. The white workers belong to the exploiting class and take part in the suppression of the blacks. The blackman is not fighting for equality with whites. Blackness is the blackman refusing to believe the whiteman's way of life is best for ... It's not a class struggle for blacks, it's a race struggle.

Gordimer's writing highlights the particular problems of being a white, but politically committed writer, in South Africa: she examines the divergent perspectives of the many different sections within South African society. Whereas Achebe identified himself with a distinctly nationalist cause, Gordimer is more problematic because she is not a member of the very group she most wants to represent in her fiction.

J.M. Coetzee

An awareness of perspectives other than the writer's own is also a central feature of J.M. Coetzee's writing. Having studied in Britain and the USA, Coetzee returned to South Africa in 1971 and is currently Professor of English at the University of Cape Town.

Coetzee's novels have been contrasted with the more explicitly realistic and political work of Gordimer, and criticised as too fictive (overtly fictional) and **allegorical,** the work of an academic. However, approaching Coetzee with an understanding of apartheid exposes the dangers of such a neat categorisation. His writing profoundly reflects the problems created by the boundaries and divides within South Africa, not least the extent to which 'meaning' (in terms of both sense/understanding and worth/value) can be found in such an environment.

His work certainly has a distinctly 'literary' quality. In *Foe* (1986), Coetzee 'rewrites' Daniel Defoe's *Robinson Crusoe* (1719). *Robinson Crusoe* is a classic colonial text, in which the hero gives a detailed account of his survival on an island. Famously, the white Crusoe develops a relationship with a native, who acts as his servant, whom he later names Friday, and who is allowed no voice in the novel.

Coetzee's narrator, however, is Crusoe's 'wife' (absent from the original), who seeks out Defoe to write her story. Such a novel could be regarded as merely a literary game, but that would be to miss the significance of such rewriting. By reworking a colonial text, Coetzee is able to call into question the assumptions and values that are embodied in it. The character named 'Cruso' in Coetzee's text makes no attempt to build a boat; his building projects can be read as the futility of empire making, a 'stupid labour'.

The novel also questions the rationale behind the writing of stories and history. Back in England, Mrs Cruso, Susan Barton, wonders, 'Are these enough strange circumstances to make a story of? How long before I am driven to invent new and stranger circumstances ...'. The reader is continually made aware of the gap between what happens and what is narrated, the reality of experience and the myths of history that are made from it.

▶ Why should questioning the myths and narratives established in colonial writing be an important aspect of post-colonial literature? How might a sceptical approach to the idea that there is one, true narrative (either fictional or historical) seem particularly apt in the context of apartheid South Africa?

It is not just the issue of how narratives are made that is examined, but by whom, and on whose behalf. It is significant that Coetzee uses the perspective of an 18th-century woman, a character in a more **marginal** position, to question the writing process.

Susan Barton ('Mrs Cruso') is continually faced with the question of how to interpret Friday's actions and moods; Friday, we have been told, has had his tongue cut out by slave traders and his silent presence permeates the novel. Whereas Gordimer includes the black voice by integrating a black perspective into her work, Coetzee uses Friday's silence to represent the exclusion of black perspectives from colonial history. Susan Barton reflects on how telling Friday's story is both essential and impossible for her:

> To tell my story and be silent on Friday's tongue is no better than offering a book for sale with pages in it quietly left empty. Yet the only tongue that can tell Friday's story is the tongue he has lost!

▶ When Coetzee wrote this novel, many black activists were banned or imprisoned. What point might he have been making about apartheid South Africa?

An awareness of context shows how the novel can be read on different levels: both as a rewriting of a colonial text and as a comment upon contemporary South Africa.

It can be argued that the problem of interpretation across boundaries is at the heart of Coetzee's work. In *Life and Times of Michael K* (1983), the central character, Michael K, lives in a world that is detached from others and indecipherable to them. Throughout the novel, South Africa is depicted as a wasteland in a state of civil war. In the passage below, Michael, having been captured by government forces, is being interviewed by the doctor in a detention camp hospital. The doctor is also the narrator in this section:

> I paused; he stared stonily back. 'Talk, Michaels,' I resumed. 'You see how easy it is to talk, now talk. Listen to me, listen how easily I fill this room with words. I know people who can talk all day without getting tired, who can fill up whole worlds talking.' Noel caught my eye but I pressed on. 'Give yourself some substance, man, otherwise you're going to slide through life absolutely unnoticed. You will be a digit in the units column at the end of the war when they make the big subtraction sum to calculate the difference, nothing more. You don't want to be simply one of the perished, do you? You want to live, don't

you? Well then, talk, make your voice heard, tell your story! ...'

Through the novel, Coetzee gives those who are the innocent victims of conflict a voice and recognises their wider significance. By narrating Michael's story, Michael, and those he represents, are given substance. As the doctor reflects: 'Michaels means something and the meaning he has is not private to me.'

As with *Foe,* the novel can be read on a number of levels: both as an allegory and as a literal story, not least because so many features of the novel (his mother's work as a domestic servant, the need for passes to move area, the detention camps) reflect very real aspects of South African experience.

However, the novel's significance can be seen in terms broader than those which reflect apartheid South Africa. It is rich in symbols which the reader can interpret and the novel conveys fundamental, one might even say, universal human needs. (See the extract in Part 3, pages 90–91.)

Post-apartheid South Africa

Since the 1994 elections swept the ANC to power and established black majority rule in South Africa, the new government has had the immense task of trying to build a country which can be united despite the atrocities of the past. Nelson Mandela has proclaimed his vision of a 'rainbow nation', a nation of opportunity for people of all races. An essential part of this process has been the need for truth about the past and for reconciliation. Mandela has himself written:

> The experience of others has taught us that nations that do not deal with the past are haunted by it for generations. The quest for reconciliation was a fundamental objective of our struggle to set up a government based on the will of the people and to build a South Africa that belongs to all.
>
> ('We should forgive but not forget', printed in *The Guardian,* 3 July 1999)

In 1995 the Truth and Reconciliation Commission (1995–1998) was established. Its functions were to investigate claims of human rights violations and provide reparation and rehabilitation for victims; importantly, it also had the power to grant amnesty to accused parties and, through the 'Register of Reconciliation', provided a forum in which perpetrators of abuses could express regret and remorse.

South African society is in a state of immense upheaval and flux. Transformations in the law and in people's attitudes mean that relationships between racial groups have been and are changing. It is this change and the problems of a new South Africa which post-apartheid writers are confronting.

Coetzee's *Disgrace* (1999)

Coetzee's most recent novel is a darkly realistic portrayal of post-apartheid South Africa. Disgraced after having an affair with a female student, David Lurie, a cultured, sophisticated academic, encounters the realities of rural life when he goes to stay with his daughter, Lucy, on her farm in the Eastern Cape. The novel is partly about his struggle to come to terms with the world in which he finds himself. The central trauma of the story is a raid on Lucy's farm, during which three black men rape her. It later becomes clear that the men were known to Lucy's neighbouring farmer, Petrus, and that one of the rapists is a member of his extended family.

Essentially, the novel explores the changing relationships between blacks and whites in the new South Africa. The issue of retribution and atonement for past atrocities features powerfully in the novel. Indeed, the relationship between races is closely examined in the light of South Africa's past. Lucy herself comes to the conclusion that rape, not theft, was the men's primary motive and that being raped might be 'the price one has to pay for staying on? Perhaps that is how they look at it; perhaps that is how I should look at it too. They see me as owing something. They see themselves as debt collectors, tax collectors ...'.

However, Coetzee offers no neat solutions or even definitions of South Africa's problems. The rape is not seen solely in terms of relations between black and white, but as part of a long history (both European and African) of male domination and violence against women. Furthermore, as *Foe* and *Life and Times of Michael K* raised the question of whites speaking on the part of blacks, so *Disgrace* questions the assumed right of men to speak on the part of women.

However, *Disgrace* affirms the responsibility of individuals to change for the better in the face of what seems a nightmare. When her father asks her if she loves the child inside her womb, Lucy replies:

'The child? No. How could I? But I will. Love will grow – one can trust Mother Nature for that. I am determined to be a good mother, David. A good mother and a good person. You should try to be a good person too.'

Such a moral novel has a particular significance in the context in which it is written. While for readers outside South Africa it may make them more aware of post-apartheid reality, for readers inside the country it perhaps attempts, as the Truth and Reconciliation Committee did, to confront atrocities and violations and still affirm the possibility of positive change.

The Caribbean

The historical and cultural context

The Caribbean is unique among the regions under discussion in that its original inhabitants, Amerindian Arawaks and Caribs, no longer inhabit the area. They were wiped out by disease and direct military oppression when Europeans began to occupy the islands in the 16th century. Though traces of Carib culture and language still exist, the Caribbean today is a mixture of the various races and cultures that have since colonised the region. This includes people and traditions from Europe, Africa, India and Asia.

Geographically, the region is an archipelago, a stretch of islands between the north eastern coast of South America and the North Atlantic Ocean. It ranges from Trinidad off the Venezuelan coast to the Bahamas, west of Miami. The British influence in the Caribbean also extended to the South American landmass in the colony of British Guiana (now Guyana).

Caribbean literature as a whole reflects a sophisticated variety of experiences, and not just within that geographical region. Through the process of migration, Caribbean culture has spread abroad, most notably to Britain. In different and often subtle ways, this sense of **diaspora** underpins much Caribbean writing.

The main focus of this section will be on the development of black writing in the Caribbean. This is certainly not to devalue other kinds of writing (writers such as V.S. Naipaul, of Indian descent, and Jean Rhys [1890–1979], of white, colonial descent, are discussed elsewhere – see pages 10 and 65), but to highlight some of the many key features of this aspect of post-colonial literature. The writers introduced come from Trinidad, Jamaica and St Lucia, and a sense of the local is reflected in much of their work. However, they also address issues which have significance throughout the Caribbean, such as the nature of colonial rule.

Early images of the Caribbean in colonial literature

The Caribbean has held a significant place in English literature from the 16th century onwards. Being the gateway to the 'New World', the islands of the Caribbean and the lands conquered on the mainland Americas fascinated the European imagination. Though writing from that early period may seem historically distant, its images have exerted a powerful influence on thinking about the Caribbean and the nature of colonisation there. Perhaps more significantly, such writing became part of a literary tradition which modern Caribbean writers would have to reinterpret, reject or rewrite from their own perspective.

On one level, these new lands seemed to represent a paradise on earth, where man lived in a state of uncorrupted innocence, as Adam and Eve had done before the Fall; for some, such as the French philosopher Montaigne (1533–1592), the discovery of native societies called into question the values of the so-called 'civilised' world. The myth of the New World as a place of untainted, rural innocence was being constructed in the European imagination. Andrew Marvell (1621–1678) used exotic images to create a sense of God's abunduce in 'Bermudas' (1653):

> He hangs in shades the orange bright,
> Like golden lamps in a green night,
> And does in the pom'ganates close
> Jewels more rich than Ormus shows.

Needless to say, such ideas and images did little to halt the conquest of the region. If anything, the land seemed there for the taking. Perhaps the most enduring and relevant depiction of colonial exploration is *The Tempest* (1611) by William Shakespeare (1564–1616). Based on accounts of a wreck off the Bermudas, it is a classic exploration of the issues which colonisation brought to the fore. These include the relationship between master and slave, the role of language in the colonising process and the nature of art and civilisation.

Sugar Islands and the creation of slave colonies

The most important factor in the creation of Caribbean societies was the establishment of plantations worked by African slaves, once the indigenous labour force had been wiped out. Their main export gained the West Indies the name of the 'Sugar Islands' and ensured that a number of white merchants accrued immense wealth. Jamaica came under British sovereignty in 1655 and became the hub of the slave trade in the area. Crucially, white Caribbean society was built upon the oppression and exploitation of black Africans, often for the purpose of supporting land and families back in England.

Some understanding of the slave trade is essential to an understanding of Caribbean literature. As well as the physical abuse involved, the process of slavery had profound effects upon the psychology and language of the transported Africans. The largest forced migration in world history, the slave trade was a process of systematic dehumanisation. Slaves on board ships were listed as 'cargo'. In the West Indies, they were catalogued and treated as working animals, even to the extent that the strongest were used to sire future workers. The trade reached its peak in the 18th century, when it is estimated that over 6,000,000 slaves were transported. The numbers are still disputed, but a conservative estimate puts the number of slaves transported across the Atlantic between 1450 and 1900 at 11,698,000. It has been estimated that fewer than half of the slaves captured actually survived the journey across the notorious 'Middle Passage'.

▶ Discuss the following questions which raise cultural issues important to Caribbean writing.

- What do you think might be the psychological effect of this mass uprooting and enslaving of peoples?

- If modern African writers could evoke a pre-colonial past in order to assert national identity, what could Caribbean writers use?

- As neither the planters nor the slaves were indigenous to the islands a unique situation arose where both, though in different ways, were aliens and exiles; how might this affect their relationship to each other?

- How might it have affected their relationship to England and the capital of empire, the '**metropolis**'?

The legacy of slavery has exerted an important influence on Caribbean writing. After its abolition in 1833, many large estates ceased to function as ex-slaves preferred subsistence farming. However, the basic structure remained the same. The vast majority of rural and urban blacks lived in poverty. Indentured (contracted) labourers were imported from India and China, and, though technically 'free', they lived in conditions which were not improved. The personal experience of poverty and a sense of its injustice would be an important force upon West Indian writers.

English in the Caribbean: standard and Creole varieties

An awareness of different kinds of language is important when approaching post-colonial Caribbean literature because it is in language that much of Caribbean history and culture is reflected. The kind of language used by a speaker or writer can reflect what kind of community s/he is from, what kind of community s/he wants to identify with, even what kind of audience s/he wants to speak to or write for. Furthermore, the question of the appropriateness or inappropriateness of different kinds of English for reflecting different kinds of Caribbean experience is one which is central when approaching this area of post-colonial literature. As with writers from India and Africa, Caribbean authors had to find a medium within English which would reflect their experience effectively.

Essentially, different types of language use distinguished landowner from enslaved. Masters and their families spoke and, importantly, wrote what has come to be described as 'standard English' (that form of English seen by the establishment to be grammatically 'correct'), while slave communities developed Creole languages. (The word 'Creole', however, has two distinct usages. It can also refer to the descendants of the first white settlers, who were born in the region. Hence the phrase 'white Creole society'.)

To state the case crudely, masters and slaves originally communicated through a simplified, functional form of English known as 'pidgin' English. Pidgins are a mixture between the two or three languages of contact, such as English and Yoruba (the language of the Yoruba ethnic group in West Africa). Creole can be seen as the development of pidgin for more extensive and intimate use, becoming eventually the dominant language of a community. Creoles are particular dialects or types of language, used by native speakers in a particular place, such as 'Jamaican English Creole'.

The use of Creole is entwined with the development of oral cultural traditions of the black slave society of the Caribbean. Until recently, Creole speakers were generally regarded by the educated as bad English speakers and the culture associated with them as unworthy of merit. Colonial schools promoted standard English and literature from England.

▶ Consider why might it have been, and might still be, so important for many Caribbean writers to use Creole in their work. What might it suggest about their intentions and the cultural tradition they seek to identify with?

The following lines are taken from Kamau Brathwaite's poem 'Dust' (1967). Two Trinidadian women are discussing a story about a volcanic eruption. ('Patois' means 'local dialect'.)

> ... Besides,
> is miles an' miles
> from the peace o' this
>
> place an' is
> alwys purrin' an' purrin'
> out smoke. Some say
> is in one o' them islands
>
> where they language tie-tongue
> an' to hear them speak so
> in they St. Lucia patois
> is as if they cahn unnerstan'
>
> a single word o' English.

▶ What does this poetry gain by being written in Creole? Consider how the speaker regards her own use 'o' English'.

The 1930s and 1940s: asserting a Caribbean identity

Political unrest and the development of nationalist politics

The West Indies suffered greatly during the economic depression of the 1930s when crop prices and wages for agricultural workers were cut. In 1937 there was rioting by Indian agricultural workers and a strike of oil workers in Trinidad and Tobago, which led to a general strike in 1938. A wave of disturbances spread through Barbados and British Guiana, and, in Jamaica, there was violent confrontation between dock workers and the police. All of these incidents, though often flaring up for local reasons, reflected a wider sense of discontent with colonial rule.

In 1944, Jamaica received a new constitution in which the governor's executive became answerable to an elected assembly of the Lower House. Jamaicans also received the right to vote for the first time. It was a pattern which would be repeated throughout most of the region.

Haile Selassie, the Rastafari movement and Marcus Garvey

In 1930 Haile Selassie was crowned Emperor of Ethiopia, and the Rastafari movement, which regarded him as the messiah, was founded in Jamaica. The popularity of Ethiopianism there, the belief in a promised land in Africa for black people as God's chosen race, can also be seen as a symptom of anti-colonial dissatisfaction.

This development coincided with Marcus Garvey's (1887–1940) 'Back to Africa' campaign of the 1920s and 1930s. Garvey was Jamaican, but was politically active in America, promoting black pride and the idea of a return to Africa.

While it is easy to underplay the importance of such influences (Garvey's Back to Africa movement was a failure in practical terms, and West Indians who were later given land in Ethiopia found themselves rejected by the indigenous community), their real significance lies in the cultural change which they represented: an emphasis on the strength of African heritage and identity, as opposed to the dominant values of European culture. Reggae music, which was to become a powerful expression of the experiences of blacks, would have a strong influence on performance poetry by, among others, Kamau Brathwaite.

C.L.R. James

By the 1930s and 1940s the established, colonial literary culture of the Caribbean was being challenged by writers who were more radically political in their outlook and who sought to identify with the black poor.

C.L.R. James (1901–1989) was both an initiator and part of the cultural changes of the 1930s and 1940s. His first work, *Triumph* (1929), is a study of 'barrack yard' (slum) life, in his own words, 'the life of ordinary people'; he concentrates on the plight of women in the yard, depicting their lives in a realistic way, which shocked contemporary readers. As with the Indian writer Mulk Raj Anand (see pages 71–73), his work is also seen as documentary or social realist.

James' novel *Minty Alley* (1936) (see Part 3, pages 92–93) was the first novel by a Caribbean writer to be published outside the West Indies. The narrator, Haynes, observes both slum life and the distance between it and himself, a young, educated intellectual. The relationship of the intellectual artist to the working class was to become an important theme in Caribbean literature.

Unlike the Rastafarian poet, Kamau Brathwaite (see pages 100–101), who was to identify himself with Africa, C.L.R. James emphasised the significance of a Western education as well as Marxist political ideas. He wrote:

> I did not learn literature from the mango tree … I set out to master the literature, philosophy and ideas of Western education. That is where I have come from and I would not pretend to be anything else … but we also became Marxists and were educated by Marxism.
>
> ('Discovering Literature in Trinidad', 1969)

James' work, as well as that of other Caribbean novelists, should be seen as part of a general rise in anti-colonial feeling in the 1930s and 1940s.

V.S. Reid

In V.S. Reid's *New Day* (1949), the narrator, John Campbell, reviews both his life and Jamaican history, from the Morant Bay uprising in 1865 to the new constitution of 1944. The Morant Bay uprising was a failed rebellion led by Paul Bogle; it was partly caused by the poverty in which ex-slaves were living, and the fact that deputations sent to England for help had been ignored. The rebellion was crushed by the execution of over 400 rebels without trial.

New Day is a fictional recreation with the emphasis on the experience of those involved. Reid's purpose is clearly influenced by the development of nationalist politics in Jamaica. In the 'Author's Note', he states that he wants to create 'as true an impression as fiction can of the way by which Jamaica and its people came by today'.

It was one of the first novels to use Creole not simply within direct speech, but for the narrative style as a whole.

▶ Read the extract from the novel (Part 3, pages 93–94) What do you think the significance was in showing history from a black Jamaican perspective? As with C.L.R. James' book, *The Black Jacobins* (1938), about the successful Haitian slave rebellion of 1814, this is sometimes called 'revisionist' history. What does that term imply to you?

Una Marson and Louise Bennett

A key part of the development of literature in the West Indies was the emergence of women's poetry, which is now among the most celebrated both locally and internationally. The two most significant poets of the period are Una Marson (1905 –1965) and Louise Bennett, both of whom were engaged with the social, political and cultural issues of their time. Both are also Jamaican.

Una Marson established the 'Caribbean Voices' programme on the BBC World Service, which became a key outlet for writing by West Indians. She was Haile Selassie's (see above) private secretary in London and was involved in The Women's International League for Peace and Freedom. In her poetry, she uses both standard English and Creole. Perhaps her most important publication is *The Moth and the Star* (1937).

Louise Bennett began performing her work publicly when she was 18 and won a scholarship to the Royal Academy of Dramatic Arts in London. On returning to Jamaica, she continued to research Jamaican folk culture between 1955 and 1959. The dramatic and folk elements of her work are particularly important.

Much of her poetry, like Una Marson's, is written in the form of **dramatic monologue** and is designed as much to be performed, as to be read privately. Her first major collection was *Dialect Verses* in 1944, followed by *Jamaica Labrish* (meaning 'gossip') in 1966; her 'Miss Lou' poems have been immensely popular throughout the Caribbean, even if critical recognition was slow in coming.

Crucially, both poets established Creole writing firmly at the centre of West Indian poetry, thus promoting a tradition of poetry linked to the oral traditions of the Caribbean, as opposed to the literary traditions of England. Louise Bennett is credited with using Creole at a level of subtlety which had not been previously achieved. (See, for example, the extract from 'Jamaica Oman' in Part 3, page 96.)

At the time, black women (particularly the poor and those without formal schooling) had a low status in much of West Indian society. The use of women's folklore and powerful female voices can be seen as a way of asserting black women's identity, character and culture.

Far from reflecting the dominant values of the age, Marson and Bennett can be seen as writing, however humorously, against a dominant male, European culture. Part of the West Indies 'problem' was considered to be the 'woman question'; women were blamed for a perceived lowering of moral standards, for high rates of pregnancy and venereal disease. The fact that many women were dependent upon a number of men because of the poverty of their conditions was not an issue.

Furthermore, black women were not depicted as naturally beautiful in the imported popular culture that influenced much West Indian society. In films and magazines, European or white American models were glamorised, with the result that straight hair and lighter skin became sought after. In this extract from 'Cinema Eyes' (1937), written by Una Marson, a mother speaks to her daughter:

> Come, I will let you go
> When black beauties
> Are chosen for the screen;
> That you may know
> Your own sweet beauty
> And not the white loveliness
> Of others for envy.

▶ In what ways might an awareness of **gender** be important when approaching the subject of Caribbean literature, and post-colonial writing in general?

Part of the importance of women's poetry can be seen in the ways that later poets such as Freddie D'Aguiar, James Berry and Grace Nichols have drawn upon female oral traditions and the use of **persona** in their writing, so that the techniques developed by Marson and Bennett are now at the centre of West Indian and black British literature.

Independence and post-independence: the political and cultural background

An initial radicalism shaped many of the political and cultural changes up to and after independence. While islands such as St Lucia (which gained semi-independence in 1967, full in 1979), remained conservative and maintained an allegiance to Britain, others, such as Jamaica and Guyana, were more nationalistic and their independence movements became increasingly confrontational.

This facilitated the rise of Black Power politics. Culturally, this meant an increased polarisation between the supposed values of blacks and whites; white literature and history were rejected as part of a growing assertion of a black identity.

However, far from being a time of liberation and renewal, for many in the Caribbean, independence has meant continued poverty, increased crime rates and political corruption. Jamaica, which gained independence in 1962, saw much economic depression in the 1970s and 1980s. The general picture is one of disillusionment as Caribbean countries have failed to establish economic independence from the United States and Britain, and therefore remain in a neo-colonial relationship, part of the Third World.

Despite the migration to Britain of a number of key writers, the two most important poets of the independence and post-independence period deliberately chose to live and work in the Caribbean. Derek Walcott, who won the Nobel Prize for Literature in 1992, and Kamau Brathwaite have both reacted in different ways to the cultural and political movements surrounding independence.

While they share similar concerns, such as the legacy of colonialism and slavery, or the nature of a Caribbean identity, both approach these subjects in different ways. As a result, they have developed distinctive voices within their poetry, which reflect the different philosophies and affiliations of each poet. Issues of history, identity and language are prominent.

Derek Walcott

During the 1950s, Walcott emphasised 'the power of the provincial' and his attachment to the Caribbean. He attended the University of the West Indies and founded Trinidad's Theatre Workshop to produce works by himself and other West Indian playwrights. His first major collection of poetry, *In a Green Night: Poems 1948–60,* appeared in 1962.

Walcott's work has been seen as the most influenced by the literary traditions of classical English poetry; it is rich in literary reference and allusion. The very title *In A Green Night* is taken from Andrew Marvell's poem 'Bermudas'. However, 'influenced' should not be taken at face value. Walcott's relationship to English literary traditions and the English language, in its various forms, is complex and challenging.

Walcott's poetry cannot easily be pigeon-holed. The impossibility of simple allegiances, whether racial or literary, can be seen as a key characteristic of his work. Consider, for example, the following lines from 'A Far Cry From Africa', a poem from his first major collection. Note how the problem of identity is closely connected to the problem of language:

> I who have cursed
> The drunken officer of British rule, how choose
> Between this Africa and the English tongue I love?

Walcott's personal history bears witness to this problem of identity. His paternal grandfather was English, his maternal one Dutch, while the women of the family were of African descent. He was born into a Protestant family on the predominantly Catholic St Lucia, which finally became a British colony as late as 1814.

Could this not be seen as one of the strengths of his position? Could this mixed origin reflect the mixed nature of the Caribbean itself?

In 'The Schooner's Flight' (1979), the narrator, Shabine, says:

> I' m just a red nigger who love the sea,
> I had a sound colonial education,

I have Dutch, Nigger, and English in me,
Either I'm nobody or I'm a nation.

Shabine, a disillusioned smuggler, but also a poet, can be seen as representing Walcott himself:

… Well, when I write
this poem, each phrase go be soaked in salt;
I go draw and knot every line as tight
as ropes in this rigging; in simple speech
my common language go be the wind,
my pages the sails of the schooner Flight.

▶ Consider how the image of the poet and his use of language are presented here. The emphasis on 'common language' perhaps gives an insight into one purpose of Walcott's poetry: that is, giving spoken Caribbean language a literary power.

In his work, Walcott uses a range of language from the French patois of his native island, to standard English, and Caribbean Creoles. The forms which he uses vary from intensely personal, lyric poems to his epic, *Omeros* (1990), a West Indian Odyssey.

Walcott's own essays on poetry reveal much about his approach to the Caribbean heritage, the history of the region. In 'The Muse of History' (1974), he rejects the aims of those writers who are controlled by, 'the fitful muse, history':

In the New World, servitude to the muse of history has produced a literature of recrimination and despair, a literature of revenge written by the descendants of slaves or a literature of remorse written by the descendants of masters … The truly tough aesthetic of the New World neither explains nor forgives history. It refuses to recognise it as a creative or culpable force.

▶ What type of literature is Walcott criticising here? What attitude to history is he advocating? How does this relate to other views you have encountered?

Walcott goes on to emphasise the importance of the New World as a place where man is 'elemental', 'Adamic', 'walking in a world without monuments or ruins'. He promotes the imagination as a means of overcoming, without denying, the legacy and scars of colonialism and independence in the Caribbean.

Kamau Brathwaite

Though from a middle class background, Brathwaite firmly rejected the values of his upbringing. In an autobiographical essay, 'Timehri' (1970), he wrote that his real education was among the boys on the beach, and that while working in Ghana he found 'my beginning ... an awareness and understanding of community, of cultural wholeness, of the place of the individual within the tribe, in society'. This personal experience is at the heart of Brathwaite's poetry.

Unlike Walcott, he embraced the Black Power politics of the 1960s. In his poetry, there is a deliberately African-centred art, employing the sounds and rhythms of what he terms 'nation language'. In his own words:

> Nation language is the language which is influenced very strongly by the African model, the African aspect of our New World/Caribbean heritage.   (from *History of the Voice*, 1979)

For Brathwaite, nation language contains elements from standard English, Creole, Rastafarian dub, jazz and blues, to negro spiritual and West African chant. The concentration is upon 'sound-effect' and the performance aspect of poetry.

His first three books (*Rights of Passage, Masks* and *Islands*) were collected together as *Arrivants: A New World Trilogy* in 1973. As a whole, the trilogy explores various African migrations, both within Africa and to the West Indies and America, through the period of the slave trade and in modern times. As such, the settings vary from a Trinidadian slum around independence to the Ashanti kingdom in West Africa before the arrival of white traders. *Arrivants* can be seen as an epic of black migration in its various forms, which links black experiences across continents and throughout different periods of history.

Brathwaite particularly emphasises African culture and history in *Masks*. Traditionally, masks are worn by African dancers when they become possessed by the spirits – often the spirits of the tribe's ancestors – that the dance invokes. This extract from *Masks* is an evocation of a ceremony of sacred drums (*Atumpan*):

> Odomankoma 'Kyerema says
> Odomankoma 'Kyerema says
> The Great Drummer of Odomankoma says
> The Great Drummer of Odomankoma says
> that he has come from sleep
> that he has come from sleep
> and is arising
> and is arising

like akoko the cock
like akoko the cock who clucks
who crows in the morning
who crows in the morning

we are addressing you
ye re kyere wo

Communicating a sense of African spirituality was so important to Brathwaite that he included a glossary of African words at the back of the book.

One of the most prominent voices in the first book, *Rights of Passage,* is Brother Man, a Rastafarian, who contrasts with the 'clean faced browns' who have lost contact with their African spiritual and cultural identity (see the extract in Part 3, pages 100–101). This emphasises Brathwaite's identification with popular black culture in its various forms.

Both Walcott and Brathwaite use the imagination as a way of making sense of the Caribbean experience and creating something positive. Their work emphasises the vastness, in terms of history, culture and geography, of that experience. This sense of variety and complex cultural transformations is a key aspect of post-colonial literature.

Assignments

Transcultural

1 What would you define as the key features of transcultural writing?

2 Read the extracts from V.S. Naipaul's *A Bend in the River* and Salman Rushdie's *Midnight's Children* (Part 3, pages 83–84 and pages 76–77). How does an awareness that such writing is transcultural affect your reading of these passages?

India

3 Select two extracts of Indian writing from Part 3 and consider how the main issues of Indian culture and history are reflected in them.

4 How important is the distinction between Indian writing before and after independence? What would you say are the main issues for writers in the pre- and post-independence periods?

5   Compare the style of two Indian writers you have read. How do the different styles reflect the different approaches and concerns of the authors?

Africa

6   Read the extracts from Achebe's *Things Fall Apart* and Soyinka's *Madmen and Specialists* (Part 3, pages 78–79 and pages 81–83). What different aspects of Nigerian experience are recreated in these pieces? How might the style and content of each passage reflect the context and purpose of the writers?

7   From your reading on the writers introduced here and the extracts given in Part 3, what would you highlight as the key features of African writing? What are the main issues to be aware of?

8   How useful do you think the label 'African writing' is when reading literature from that continent?

9   After reading the extracts in this section and in Part 3, pages 89–90 and pages 90–91, think carefully about Gordimer and Coetzee's responses to apartheid. What aspects of the tone and style of each passage would you use to support your ideas?

Caribbean

10 Compare the portrayal of Trinidadian life in the extracts from C.L.R. James' *Minty Alley* and V.S. Naipaul's *Miguel Street* (Part 3, pages 92–93 and 97–98). How might the differences in tone and style reflect the different predicaments and purposes of the authors?

11 Compare the ways in which women are presented by male and female Caribbean writers.

12 Caribbean literature is often seen as the writing of rootlessness and diaspora. How important are these issues in the writers you have read?

13 Much Caribbean writing deals with the trauma of slavery and deprivation. Consider the different ways Caribbean writers have responded to a history of black suffering.

2 | Approaching the texts

- What are the key issues for the reader of post-colonial literature?

- How might the various styles of post-colonial writing be bound up with issues of perspective and identity?

- How does post-colonial literature reflect a range of indigenous and colonial influences?

While the purpose of Part 1 was to provide a sense of writers in their different contexts, the purpose of Part 2: Approaching the texts is to focus on issues relating to the reading of post-colonial literature. As such, this section builds on Part 1, while encouraging a more comparative approach both within and between writers, texts and regions.

Though it is only possible to discuss some of the different ways in which post-colonial writers have responded to key issues, an awareness of them is essential when approaching post-colonial texts. They include the use of **indigenous** cultural ① traditions, the appropriation of English, and the impact (whether cultural, ③ psychological or political) of colonialism and its aftermath.

However, beneath these lie broader questions about the problem of identity and ④ perspective in post-colonial writing, as well as the problem of how to approach a genre which is relatively new, and which may contain elements that are unfamiliar, ⑤ and may even seem inaccessible, to the reader.

The reader clearly has an important role when approaching the texts; not least because where one places one's focus as a reader influences how one writes about post-colonial literature. One purpose of this section is to clarify what the key areas of focus might be, and also to encourage the reader to think critically about the ideas and propositions offered.

The use of indigenous traditions

It has been argued that post-colonial writing is part of a process whereby native writers reject the English culture, promoted in schools and colleges across the empire, and reassert the indigenous culture to which they belong. Rather than trying to imitate the literature of their colonial masters, such writers gain strength from tapping into native, often oral, traditions.

In this brief extract from *The Wretched of the Earth* (1961), the Algerian thinker, Franz Fanon (1925–1961), outlines a transformation in the role of the writer, who begins to identify more with the culture of the people:

> While at the beginning the native intellectual used to produce his work to be read exclusively by the oppressor, whether with the intention of charming him or of denouncing him ... now the native writer progressively takes on the habit of addressing his own people ... On another level, the oral tradition, stories, epics, and songs of the people – which formerly were filed away as set pieces are now beginning to change ...
>
> (translated from the French)

These lines are a reminder of the importance of indigenous traditions as a way of asserting identity in opposition to the colonial culture. When approaching post-colonial texts, a useful question to ask is: to what extent does the use of indigenous traditions shape the language and focus of the text?

▶ Read the extract from *The Famished Road* by the Nigerian writer Ben Okri (Part 3, pages 86–87). The narrator is an *abiku*. In Yoruba mythology an *abiku* is a spirit-child who is destined to die and be reborn continually, belonging more to the spirit world than earthly reality. His father and his companion, Ade, another *abiku,* are dying.

    What words or phrases indicate that Okri is drawing upon Yoruba traditions? How does that shape the perspective of the passage? How does it affect your experience as a reader?

▶ The Fanon extract also raises the question of the writer's audience. What does the fact that Okri is writing in English, which can only be read by a minority of Nigerians, suggest about his intended audience?

    Reread the passage and note what traditions, other than Yoruba, Okri uses. What might this suggest about the author's approach to indigenous culture?

Now consider the following stage directions from Wole Soyinka's *The Lion and the Jewel*. The use of mime and dance is an integral part of traditional street theatre in West Africa:

> A terrific shout and a clap of drums. Lakunle enters the spirit of the dance with enthusiasm. He takes over from Sidi, stations his cast all over the stage as the jungle, leaves the right topstage clear for four girls who are to dance the motor-car. A mime follows the visitor's entry into Ilujinle, and his short stay among the villagers. Four girls crouch on the floor, as four wheels of a car. Lakunle directs their spacing, then takes his place in the middle and sits on air. He alone

does not dance. He does realistic miming. Soft throbbing of drums, gradually swelling in volume, and the four 'wheels' begin to rotate the upper halves of their bodies in perpendicular circles.

▶ Why might Soyinka have wished to incorporate these stage directions into the play? What does it suggest about the cultural tradition with which he seeks to identify?

Approaching post-colonial texts, an awareness of how audiences/readers from different cultural contexts might respond helps create an understanding of how texts might have a different significance in different environments.

▶ Reflect briefly on the different ways West African audiences and English audiences might respond to this kind of theatre. How might indigenous traditions have a different significance for readers both inside and outside the cultures from which they originate?

The use of indigenous traditions can take many forms, in prose, drama or poetry. However, it would clearly be an over-simplification to see post-colonial writing purely in terms of a rejection of the culture of the coloniser in favour of indigenous traditions. All writers have their own relationship to colonising and indigenous traditions, depending upon personal experience, artistic aims and the context within which they write. Approaching post-colonial texts, it is important to be sensitive to the different levels of influence within the writing because these can reflect the cultural experience of a writer, but also because they reflect the sophisticated set of influences that make up post-colonial literature.

The appropriation of English

A vital issue when approaching post-colonial texts is how the English language has been adapted by post-colonial writers. Because native writers were using a medium that was a foreign language and did not naturally reflect the culture and experiences that they wished to convey, they have had to shape it to suit their purposes.

It can be argued that this process has a political and psychological dimension. It is political because changing of the language of the colonial master can be seen to symbolise a refusal to be dominated by the culture of that master. The psychological significance lies in the fact that shaping a language to one's own needs shows a confidence, a feeling of ownership and gives a sense of empowerment to the user.

political

psychological

▶ Read the extracts from Chinua Achebe's *Things Fall Apart* and Raja Rao's *Kanthapura* (Part 3, pages 78–79 and 73–74) and reflect on how each writer has appropriated English. You should focus on: vocabulary, rhythm, tone and the extent to which the passages seem to utilise oral traditions.

What do you consider to be the main problems for the reader when encountering such texts for the first time?

How might experiencing unfamiliar vocabulary, setting or ideas be an important part of reading post-colonial literature?

While some writers have appropriated standard English, others, such as writers from the Caribbean, have had an alternative English in the form of Creole which they could utilise. This is different from appropriation because Creoles have their own already established grammar.

In the following lines from James Berry's 'Lucy's Letter' (1982), the speaker of the poem is an immigrant Caribbean woman to Britain. ('Labrish' means 'gossip'.)

> Things harness me here. I long
> for we labrish bad. Doors
> not fixed open here.
> No Leela either. No Cousin
> Lil, Miss Lottie or Bro'-Uncle.
> Dayclean doesn't have cockcrowin'
> Midmornin' doesn' bring
> Cousin-Maa with her naseberry tray ...

▶ How does the use of Creole create the mood of the poem and help to emphasise the predicament of the speaker?

However, as with the use of indigenous traditions, the reader should be wary of accepting simple formulas. Numerous post-colonial writers, such as V.S. Naipaul and Michael Ondaatje, use standard English as their main medium of expression. Earlier, M.R. Anand and C.L.R. James used standard English as a medium through which to criticise the effects of colonialism and the conditions of colonised peoples.

Post-colonial literature and the English canon

Though indigenous traditions have played an extremely important part in the development of post-colonial literature, the role of English literature and the English **canon** also needs to be kept in mind when approaching post-colonial texts.

Post-colonial writing often refers to, replies to or echoes texts which were significant in the colonial period. Though post-colonial writers have developed their own traditions, they have achieved that partly through recreating the literature inherited through empire.

Consider the following epigraph (opening quotation) from Chinua Achebe's *Things Fall Apart*. It is taken from the poem,' The Second Coming', by the Irish poet W.B. Yeats (1865–1935), and gives the novel its title:

Turning and turning in the widening gyre
The falcon cannot bear the falconer;
Things fall apart; the centre cannot hold;
Mere anarchy is loosed upon the world.

Achebe has said that he wrote the novel in order to reassert African identity and as part of the growth of Nigerian nationalism, yet he has used a reference to a poem considered an important work in the English literary canon (an ironic fact given Yeats' own commitment to Irish nationalism).

Read the wording of the epigraph carefully. What significance might the quotation have had for Achebe, writing at a point when the British were losing their empire in Africa? The novel is partly about the disruption of Ibo society by missionaries and colonialists: in that context might it not also refer to the break up of traditional African society and the consequences of that?

▶ Think about the significance of Achebe using the Yeats poem (based on the Christian belief of the end of the world and the second coming of Christ) in an African context. Consider how the context might change the meaning of the quotation itself.

'Rewriting' the canon

Read the following passages. The first, set in England, is from *Jane Eyre* (1847) by Charlotte Brontë. In it, Mr Rochester admits to already being married, when his wedding to Jane is interrupted by Mr Mason and his solicitor, Mr Briggs:

> "... Some have whispered to you that she is my bastard half-sister; some, my cast off mistress; – I now inform you that she is my wife, whom I married fifteen years ago, – Bertha Mason by name; sister of the resolute personage, who is now, with his quivering limbs and white cheeks, showing you what a stout heart men can bear. Cheer up, Dick! – never fear me! – I'd almost as soon strike a woman as you. Bertha Mason is mad; and she came of a mad family: – idiots and maniacs through three generations! Her mother, the Creole, was both a mad woman and a drunkard! – as I found out after I had wed the daughter; for they were silent on family secrets before. Bertha, like a dutiful child, copied her parents in both points ..."

The second passage, set on an unnamed honeymoon island off Jamaica, is from *Wide Sargasso Sea* (1966) by Jean Rhys. The novel is a prequel to *Jane Eyre* and the story of the first Mrs Rochester. Jean Rhys was a white Caribbean Creole (in this case, someone born in the Caribbean as opposed to someone who migrates there).

Antoinette Rochester (named Bertha by her husband) is speaking to her husband, the narrator here:

> "You want to know about my mother, I will tell you about her, the truth, not lies." Then she was silent for so long that I said gently, "I know that after your father died, she was very lonely and unhappy."
>
> "And very poor," she said. "Don't forget that. For five years. Isn't it quick to say. And isn't it long to live. And lonely. She was so lonely that she grew away from other people. That happens. It happened to me too but it was easier for me because I hardly remember anything else. For her it was strange and frightening. And then she was so lovely. I used to think that every time she looked in the glass she must have hoped and pretended. I pretended too. Different things of course. You can pretend for a long time but one day it falls away and you are alone … It was an old-time house and once there was an avenue of royal palms but a lot of them had fallen and others had been cut down and the ones that were left looked lost. Lost trees. Then they poisoned her horse and she could not ride any more …"

▶ How does your reading of the second passage alter your response to the first?

▶ How does an awareness that Rhys is 'rewriting' a text from the English canon affect your appreciation of her writing?

Seeing these two extracts side by side raises the question whether *Wide Sargasso Sea* can (or should) be read as an independent text or whether its full significance can only be appreciated if it is read in relation to *Jane Eyre*.

In *Jane Eyre*, the Caribbean only features in the margins of the novel, but it is where the majority of *Wide Sargasso Sea* is set. In *Jane Eyre*, the mad woman never communicates her position verbally; she is either an ominous presence or depicted as depraved, but, in the Rhys' novel, she articulates her position.

Articulating the position of those marginalised in classic English texts is a key aspect of post-colonial writing; and the 'decentering' or 'relocating' away from the metropolis, which can be created through rewriting, is an essential part of that process.

Gender

An awareness of gender is important when approaching post-colonial texts because women have had experiences very different from those of men in the colonial and post-colonial world. The growing awareness of women's writing and of its importance has been an integral part of the development of post-colonial literature and provides an important perspective within the genre.

The experience of women within empire was often one of double oppression. Whereas colonised men had to be subservient to their colonial masters, colonised women often had to be subservient to both their colonial masters and to the **patriarchal** nature of their own societies. For the most part, empire itself was strongly patriarchal, so that women from both the colonising and the colonised groups were marginalised and controlled.

However, when approaching post-colonial writing the reader should be aware of how different the portrayal of women in different regions, from different classes and at different times can be. This diversity is important as it emphasises the distinctive and individual nature of women's experiences.

The following passage is taken from Tsitsi Dangarembga's *Nervous Conditions* (1988), which is set in Rhodesia (now Zimbabwe) in the 1960s. The novel explores the position of women in a modern African society influenced both by traditional and European values, and firmly within the context of colonialism. Tambudzai has just won a scholarship to an exclusive convent school, but her uncle, Babamukuru, an African headmaster and with whom she is living, has the following objections:

> 'It is not a question of money,' he assured me. 'Although there would still be a lot of expense on my part, you have your scholarship, so the major financial burden would be lifted. But I feel that even that little money could be better used. For one thing, there is now the small boy at home. Every month I put away a little bit, a very little bit, a very little bit every month, so that when he is of school-going age everything will be provided for. As you know, he is the only boy in your family, so he must be provided for. As for you, we think we are providing for you quite well. By the time you have finished your Form Four you will be able to take your course, whatever it is that you choose. In time you will be earning money. You will be in a position to be married by a decent man and set up a decent home. In all that we are doing for you, we are preparing you for this future life of yours, and I have observed from my own daughter's behaviour that it is not a good thing for a young girl to associate too much with these white people, to have too much freedom. I have seen that girls who do that do not develop into decent women.'

▶ How does the passage depict the position of Western educated women in black Rhodesian society? What assumptions and values are held by Babamukuru?

▶ The issue of gender raises the important question of whether writing by women should be approached as intrinsically different from writing by men. Reread the lines from 'Lucy's Letter' by James Berry (page 64) in which a male writer uses a female persona. Is the poem any less authentic or effective because it has been written by a male author? Consider how you might approach the poem differently if it had been written by a woman or was autobiographical.

The importance of gender-based approaches to post-colonial literature reflects a growing awareness of the need for women to determine how they are represented and to assert their own histories and cultures.

▶ Think again about the extract from Jean Rhys' *Wide Sargasso Sea*. How might an awareness of gender issues affect your response to it?

The range of texts within post-colonial writing

Approaching individual post-colonial texts, the reader has the difficult task of appreciating not just what is distinctive and individual, but also seeing how that text is part of the broader genre of post-colonial literature. In other words, how has the writer responded to the key issues of post-colonial literature?

Asking this question about individual texts, whether whole works or extracts, can provide a useful framework for analysis. When comparing texts, it can help to highlight important similarities and differences; these may reflect both the authors' individual artistic aims and the cultural experiences which go to shape their work, the particular contexts from which they are writing. Approaching post-colonial texts, an awareness of the issues raised in this section, combined with a sense of context, will help to 'open up' the works themselves.

Assignments

1   Without being limited to the issues raised in Part 2, what would you say should be the main areas of focus when approaching post-colonial texts? How are these areas of focus reflected in the language of the text(s) you are studying?

2   Keep a reading journal in which you note initial impressions of the post-colonial texts you are reading. What are the key issues for you personally when encountering post-colonial literature? How would you describe the psychological, imaginative experience of reading post-colonial literature?

3   How useful do you find Fanon's model (pages 61–62): that post-colonial writing is part of a rejection of the culture of the coloniser in favour of oral traditions?

4   Research, if appropriate, the relevant indigenous traditions to the text(s) you are studying. These could be literary, oral, religious or artistic traditions referred to in the text(s). How does a knowledge of traditional culture affect or enhance your appreciation of the literature?

3 | Texts and extracts

The texts and extracts that follow have been chosen to illustrate key themes and points made elsewhere in the book, and to provide material which may be useful when working on the tasks and assignments in Parts 1, 2 and 4. The first extract offers an example of colonial writing; subsequent extracts are organised by region.

Colonial writing

Joseph Conrad   cf. 'Discourse'
p. 104-5

From 'Heart of Darkness' (1902)

The narrator, Marlow, recounts his journey in search of Kurtz, a colonial agent of high renown, who lives at the 'Inner Station'. The novella is set in the Belgian Congo where Conrad himself captained a steam boat.

> The word ivory would ring in the air for a while – and on we went again into the silence, along empty reaches, round the still bends, between the high walls of our winding way, reverberating in hollow claps the ponderous beat of the stern-wheel. Trees, trees, millions of trees, massive, immense, running up high; and at their foot, hugging the bank against the stream, crept the little begrimed steamboat, like a sluggish beetle crawling on the floor of a lofty portico. It made you feel very small, very lost, and yet it was not altogether depressing, that feeling. After all, if you were small, the grimy beetle crawled on – which was just what you wanted it to do. Where the pilgrims imagined it crawled to I don't know. To some place where they expected to get something, I bet! For me it crawled towards Kurtz – exclusively; but when the steam-pipes started leaking we crawled very slow. The reaches opened before us and closed behind, as if the forest had stepped leisurely across the water to bar the way for our return. We penetrated deeper and deeper into the heart of darkness. It was very quiet there. At night sometimes the roll of drums behind the curtain of trees would run up the river and remain sustained faintly, as if hovering in the air high over our heads, till the first break of day. Whether it meant war, peace, or prayer we could not tell. The dawns were heralded by the descent of a chill stillness; the wood-cutters slept, their fires burned low; the snapping of a twig would

make you start. We were wanderers on prehistoric earth, on an earth that wore the aspect of an unknown planet. We could have fancied ourselves the first of men taking possession of an accursed inheritance, to be subdued at the cost of profound anguish and of excessive toil. But suddenly, as we struggled round a bend, there would be a glimpse of rush walls, of peaked grass-roofs, a burst of yells, a whirl of black limbs, a mass of hands clapping, of feet stamping, of bodies swaying, of eyes rolling, under the droop of heavy and motionless foliage. The steamer toiled along slowly on the edge of a black and incomprehensible frenzy. The prehistoric man was cursing us, praying to us, welcoming us – who could tell? We were cut off from the comprehension of our surroundings; we glided past like phantoms, wondering and secretly appalled, as sane men would be before an enthusiastic outbreak in a madhouse. We could not understand because we were too far and could not remember, because we were travelling in the night of first ages, of those ages that are gone, leaving hardly a sign – and no memories.

The earth seemed unearthly. We are accustomed to look upon the shackled form of a conquered monster, but there – there you could look at a thing monstrous and free. It was unearthly, and the men were – No, they were not inhuman. Well, you know, that was the worst of it – this suspicion of their not being inhuman. It would come slowly to one. They howled and leaped, and spun, and made horrid faces; but what thrilled you was just the thought of their humanity – like yours – the thought of your remote kinship with this wild and passionate uproar. Ugly. Yes, it was ugly enough; but if you were man enough you would admit to yourself that there was in you just the faintest trace of a response to the terrible frankness of that noise, a dim suspicion of there being a meaning in it which you – you so remote from the night of first ages – could comprehend.

India

Mulk Raj Anand

From *Coolie* (1936)

Coolie depicts the life of Munoo, an orphan boy. Here, Munoo begins his weekly work at an English-owned Bombay cotton mill. Hari is a devout Hindu, who has given Munoo shelter with his family. Ratan is a trade unionist.

It is difficult enough for anyone to face a Monday morning. It was like doomsday to the coolies, especially after they had lost themselves in the ecstasy of human relationships for a day and regained their souls.

But on Monday mornings they returned to work. On Monday mornings they faced death again. And, as if the monster of death were some invisible power which throttled them as soon as they set out to work, they walked to the factory in a kind of hypnotised state of paralysis, in a state of apathy and torpor which made the masks of their faces assume the sinister horror of unexpressed pain.

'Why are they sad?' Munoo wondered, because he still had a little of the stored-up vitality of his youth left in him. And he stared hard at them. Shivering, weak, bleary, with twisted, ugly faces, black, filthy, gutless, spineless, they stole along with unconscious, not-there looks; idiots, looking at the smoky heavens as they signed or murmured 'Ram Ram' and other names of God in greeting to each other and in thanksgiving for the gifts of the Almighty. The boy recalled how his patron Prabha in Daulatpur used to say that everything was the blessing of God, even Ganpat's ill treatment, the beating the police had given him and the fever of which he nearly died – that all suffering was the result of our having committed evil deeds. Perhaps these people also believed in Karma. Hari, indeed, had often said so, and he had hoped that one day his luck would turn, because he had done some good deeds in his life. Ratan laughed at all such wisdom, and he alone went light-heartedly through life; with a brave, handsome face, beaming with smiles, he alone went with a pride and a swagger, while the other coolies cringed with humility.

Munoo felt a superstitious awe for Ratan's fate. An overpowering sense of doom crept into his soul as he thought of him. He tried to dismiss his thoughts by repeating the Indian phrase: 'I must not think of Ratan as handsome and lucky, lest my evil eye bring bad luck to him.' But, as if his thoughts were echo-auguries, the smile on the wrestler's face faded one morning.

It was the Chimta Sahib's habit to stand by the door of the preparing-shed every morning to exact salaams and other forms of homage from the coolies. A flourish of the hand, a curse, an oath or abuse was the greeting he offered in exchange. This conduct was well suited to the preservation of peace in the mill, as even the sight of his big, beefy body cowed the coolies and put the fear of God into them, and they were then in the right frame of mind to perform their duties. Occasionally he kicked a coolie. But that was when he had got drunk early or quarrelled with Mrs Thomas, and sometimes it was when he had read in the morning paper the news of a nationalist demonstration, a terrorist outrage or an attempt at seditious communist propaganda which he, as a member of the British race of India, considered to be more a personal affront than the pursuit of an ideal of freedom on the part of the exploited. He had long since forgotten the days during which he himself had eked out a miserable existence in Lancashire.

Ratan was rather an independent-minded person. He did not bow down to salaam the foreman. He had the confidence of his own personal strength and, behind that, the strength of the Union. He knew he was a good worker and deserved full pay at the end of the month. And when his pay was not forthcoming at the time when it was due, or when he was threatened with a cut for damaged cloth or for being late, he agitated.

Raja Rao

From *Kanthapura* (1938)

The narrator is an old woman from Kanthapura village. Set during a *Kartik* religious festival (the festival of the Hindu god, Kartikeya, son of Shiva), this passage depicts a *satyagraha* demonstration in response to the arrest of Moorthy, the novel's Gandhi figure.

And then men rush from this street and that street, and the Police Inspector seeing this hesitates before coming down, and Rachanna barks out again, 'Mahatma Gandhi ki jai!' And the Police Inspector shouts, 'Arrest that swine!' and when they come to arrest him, everybody gets round him and says, 'No, we'll not give him up'. And the Police Inspector orders, 'Give them a licking,' and from this side and that there is the bang of the lathi and men shriek and women weep and the children begin to cry and groan, and more and more men go forward towards Moorthy, and more policemen beat them, and then Moorthy says something to the Police Inspector and the Police Inspector nods his head, and Moorthy comes along the veranda and says 'Brothers!' and there is such a silence that the Kartik lights glow brighter. 'Brothers, in the name of the Mahatma, let there be peace and love and order. As long as there is a God in Heaven and purity in our hearts evil cannot touch us. We hide nothing. We hurt none. And if these gentlemen want to arrest us, let them. Give yourself up to them. That is the true spirit of the Satyagrahi. The Mahatma' – here the Police Inspector drags him back brutally, but Moorthy continues – The Mahatma has often gone to prison ...' – and the Police Inspector gets so angry at this, that he gives a slap on Moorthy's face, but Moorthy stands firm and says nothing. Then suddenly Rachanna shouts out from below, 'Mahatma Gandhi ki jai! Come, brothers, come!' and he rushes up the steps towards Moorthy, and suddenly, in sinister omen, all the Kartik lights seemed quenched, clay pots and candelabras and banana trunks and house after house became dark, and something so sinister kicked our backs that we all rush up behind Rachanna crying, 'Mahatma Gandhi ki jai!' and now the police catch Rachanna and the one behind him and the one behind the one who was behind him, and they spit on them and bind them with ropes, while at the other end of the courtyard is seen Rangamma, Badè Khan beside her. Then the Police Inspector thinks this is the right time to come down, for the lights were all out and the leaders all arrested, and as Moorthy is being dragged down the steps Rachanna's wife and Madanna's wife and Sampanna's wife and Papamma and Sankamma and Veeramma come forward and cry out, 'Oh, give us back our men and our master, our men and our master,' but the Police Inspector says, 'Give them a shoe-shower,' and the policemen kick them in the back and on the head and in the stomach, and while Rachanna's wife is crying, Madanna's wife is squashed against a wall and her breasts squeezed.

R.K. Narayan

From *The English Teacher* (1945)

Towards the end of the novel, Krishnan, the narrator, decides to resign from his teaching post at Albert Mission College, Malgudi.

My mind was made up. I was in search of a harmonious existence and everything that disturbed that harmony was to be rigorously excluded, even my college work. One whole night I sat up in the loneliness of my house thinking it over, and before the night was out my mind was made up. I could not go on with that work; nor did I need the one hundred rupees they gave me. At first I had thought of sending in my resignation by letter to Brown, and making an end of it. I would avoid all the personal contacts, persuasions, and all the possible sentimentalities inevitable in the act of snapping familiar roots. I would send in a letter which would be a classic in its own way, and which would singe the fingers of whoever touched it. In it I was going to attack a whole century of false education. I was going to explain why I could no longer stuff Shakespeare and Elizabethan metre and Romantic poetry for the hundredth time into young minds and feed them on the dead mutton of literary analysis and theories and histories, while what they needed was lessons in the fullest use of the mind. This education had reduced us to a nation of morons; we were strangers to our own culture and camp followers of another culture, feeding on leavings and garbage.

After coffee I sat down at my table with several sheets of large paper before me. I began 'Dear Mr Brown: This is my letter of resignation. You will doubtless want to know the reasons. Here they are ...' I didn't like this. It was too breezy. I scored it out and began again. I filled three sheets, and reading it over, felt ashamed of myself. It was too theatrical and pompous for my taste. I was entangled too much in theories and platitudes and holding forth to all whom it might concern. It was like a rabid attack on all English writers, which was hardly my purpose. 'What fool could be insensible to Shakespeare's sonnets or the "Ode to the West Wind" or "A thing of beauty is a joy for ever"?' I reflected. 'But what about examinations and critical notes? Didn't these largely take the place of literature? What about our own roots?' I thought over it deeply and felt very puzzled. I added: 'I am up against the system, the whole method and approach of a system of education which makes us morons, cultural morons, but efficient clerks for all your business and administrative offices. You must not think that I am opposed to my particular studies of authors ...' The repetition of ideas uttered a hundred times before. It looked like a rehash of an article entitled 'Problems of Higher Education', which appeared again and again in a weekend educational supplement – the yarn some 'educationist' was spinning out for ten rupees a column.

'This is not what I want to say,' I muttered to myself and tore up the letter and stuffed it into the wastepaper basket. 'There is something far deeper that I wish to say.'

I took out a small sheet of paper and wrote: 'Dear Sir, I beg to tender my resignation for personal reasons. I request you to relieve me immediately ...' I put it in an envelope.

Salman Rushdie

From *Midnight's Children* (1981)

Towards the end of the novel, the narrator, Saleem Sinai, reflects upon the impact of Indira Gandhi's sterilisation programme on India's 'midnight's children', the children of independence.

They were good doctors: they left nothing to chance. Not for us the simple vas- and tubectomies performed on the teeming masses; because there was a chance, just a chance that such operations could be reversed ... ectomies were performed, but irreversibly: testicles were removed from sacs, and wombs vanished for ever.

Test- and hysterectomised, the children of midnight were denied the possibility of reproducing themselves ... but that was only a side-effect, because they were truly extraordinary doctors, and they drained us of more than that: hope, too, was excised, and I don't know how it was done, because the numbers had marched over me, I was out for the count, and all I can tell you is that at the end of eighteen days on which the stupefying operations were carried out at a mean rate of 23.33 per day, we were not only missing little balls and inner sacs, but other things as well: in this respect, I came off better than most, because drainage-above had robbed me of my midnight-given telepathy, I had nothing to lose, the sensitivity of a nose cannot be drained away ... but as for the rest of them, for all those who had come to the palace of the wailing widows with their magical gifts intact, the awakening from anaesthesia was cruel indeed, and whispering through the wall came the tale of their undoing, the tormented cry of children who had lost their magic: she had cut it out of us, gorgeously with wide rolling hips she had devised the operation of our annihilation, and now we were nothing, who were we, a mere 0.00007 per cent, now fishes could not be multiplied nor base metals transmuted; gone forever, the possibilities of flight and lycanthropy and the originally-one-thousand-and one marvellous promises of a numinous midnight.

Drainage below: it was not a reversible operation.

Who were we? Broken promises; made to be broken.

And now I must tell you about the smell.

Yes, you must have all of it: however overblown, however Bombay-talkie-melodramatic, you must let it sink in, you must see! What Saleem smelled in the evening of January 18th, 1977: something frying in an iron skillet, soft unspeakable somethings spiced with turmeric coriander cumin and fenugreek ... the pungent inescapable fumes of what-had-been-excised, cooking over a low, slow fire.

When four-hundred-and-twenty suffered ectomies, an avenging Goddess ensured that certain ectomised parts were curried with onions and green chillies, and fed to the pie-dogs of Benares. (There were four hundred and twenty-one ectomies performed: because one of us, whom we called Narada or Markandaya, had the ability of changing sex; he, or she, had to be operated on twice.)

No, I can't prove it, not any of it. Evidence went up in smoke: some was fed to pie-dogs; and later, on March 20th, files were burned by a mother with particoloured hair and her beloved son.

Anita Desai

From *In Custody* (1984)

Deven, a teacher of Hindi, has come to interview Nur, a famous Urdu poet, at the poet's house in Delhi.

The house was very still, miraculously silent. The tall hospital walls cut it off from the hubbub of the bazaar, Deven supposed. All he could hear were the pigeons complaining to and consoling each other up on the dusty ledges of the high skylights, and the laboured sound of the poet's breath, snarled in his throat with some elderly phlegm.

'Urdu poetry?' he finally sighed, turning a little to one side, towards Deven although not actually addressing himself to a person, merely to a direction, it seemed. 'How can there be Urdu poetry when there is no Urdu language left? It is dead, finished. The defeat of the Moghuls by the British threw a noose over its head, and the defeat of the British by the Hindi-wallahs tightened it. So now you see its corpse lying here, waiting to be buried.' He tapped his chest with one finger.

'No, sir, please don't talk like that,' Deven said eagerly, perspiration breaking out on his upper lip and making it glisten. 'We will never allow that to happen. That is why Murad is publishing his journal. And the printing press where it is published is for printing Urdu books, sir. They are getting large orders even today. And my college – it is only a small college, a private college outside Delhi – but is has a department of Urdu –'

'Do you teach there?' A wrinkled eyelid moved, like a turtle's, and a small, quick eye peered out at Deven as if at a tasty fly.

Deven shrank back in apology. 'No, sir, I teach in – in the Hindi department. I took my degree in Hindi because –'

But the poet was not listening. He was laughing and spitting as he laughed because he did it so rustily and unwillingly. Phlegm flew. 'You see,' he croaked, 'what did I tell you? Those Congress-wallahs have set up Hindi on top as our ruler. You are its slave. Perhaps a spy even if you don't know it, sent to the universities to destroy whatever remains of Urdu, hunt it out and kill it. And you tell me it is for an Urdu magazine you wish to interview me. If so, why are you teaching Hindi?' he suddenly roared, fixing Deven with that small, turtle-lidded eye that had now become lethal, a bullet.

'I studied Urdu, sir, as a boy, in Lucknow. My father, he was a schoolteacher, a scholar, and a lover of Urdu poetry. He taught me the language. But he died. He died and my mother brought me to Delhi to live with her relations here. I was sent to the nearest school, a Hindi-medium school, sir,' Deven stumbled through the explanation, 'I took my degree in Hindi, sir, and now I am temporary lecturer in Lala Ram Lal College at Mirpore. It is my living, sir. You see I am a married man, a family man. But I still remember my lessons in Urdu, how my father taught me, how he used to read poetry to me. If it were not for the need to earn a living, I would – I would –' Should he tell him his aspirations, scribbled down on pieces of paper and hidden between the leaves of his books?

'Oh, earning a living?' mocked the old man as Deven struggled visibly with his diffidence. 'Earning a living comes first, does it? Why not trade in rice and oil if it is a living you want to earn?'

Crushed, Deven's shoulders sagged. 'I am – only a teacher, sir,' he murmured, 'and must teach to support my family. But poetry – Urdu – these are – one needs, I need to serve them to show my appreciation. I cannot serve them as you do –'

Africa

Chinua Achebe

From *Things Fall Apart* (1958)

Set in Umuofia, an Ibo village, the passage introduces Unoka, the artistic but lazy father of Okonkwo, the novel's hero. Okoye has come to Unoka to demand the repayment of cowries he has lent him. (An *ogene* is a gong-like instrument.)

Having spoken plainly so far, Okoye said the next half a dozen sentences in proverbs. Among the Ibo the art of conversation is regarded very highly, and proverbs are the palm-oil with which words are eaten. Okoye was a great talker and he spoke for a long time, skirting round the subject and then hitting it finally. In short, he was asking Unoka to return the two hundred cowries he had borrowed from him more than two years before. As soon as Unoka understood what his friend was driving at, he burst out laughing. He laughed loud and long and his voice rang out clear as the ogene, and tears stood in his eyes. His visitor was amazed, and sat speechless. At the end, Unoka was able to give an answer between fresh outbursts of mirth.

'Look at that wall,' he said, pointing at the far wall of his hut, which was rubbed with red earth so that it shone. 'Look at those lines of chalk;' and Okoye saw groups of short perpendicular lines drawn in chalk. There were five groups, and the smallest group had ten lines. Unoka had a sense of the dramatic and so he allowed a pause, in which he took a pinch of snuff and sneezed noisily, and then he continued: 'Each group there represents a debt to someone, and each stroke is one hundred cowries. You see, I owe that man a thousand cowries. But he has not come to wake me up in the morning for it. I shall pay you, but not today. Our elders say that the sun will shine on those who stand before it shines on those who kneel under them. I shall pay my big debts first.' And he took another pinch of snuff, as if that was paying the big debts first. Okoye rolled his goatskin and departed.

When Unoka died he had taken no title at all and he was heavily in debt. Any wonder then that his son Okonkwo was ashamed of him? Fortunately, among these people a man was judged according to his worth and not according to the worth of his father. Okonkwo was clearly cut out for great things. He was still young but he had won fame as the greatest wrestler in the nine villages. He was a wealthy farmer and had two barns full of yams, and had just married his third wife. To crown it all he had taken two titles and had shown incredible prowess in two inter-tribal wars. And so although Okonkwo was still young, he was already one of the greatest men of his time. Age was respected among his people, but achievement was revered. As the elders said, if a child washed his hands he could eat with kings. Okonkwo had clearly washed his hands and so he ate with kings and elders. And that was how he came to look after the doomed lad who was sacrificed to the village of Umuofia by their neighbours to avoid war and bloodshed. The ill-fated lad was called Ikemefuna.

Ngugi wa Thiong'o

From *A Grain of Wheat* (1967)

Set in Yala detention camp, during Mau Mau, this passage conveys the experience
of Gikonyo, who has been imprisonned by the British. Thabai is his home village
and Mumbi is his wife. Gatu has been regarded by the other prisoners as their 'good
spirit', binding them against the British so that they will not confess their Mau Mau
oaths.

The soldiers came for Gatu in the quarry. That very evening the others
found his body hanging against the wall of his cell. 'Hanged himself
…' the commandant told them, laughing. 'Guilt, you see! Unless you
confess, you'll end up like him.' Gloom fell on Yala. They could not
agree on a common united response to Gatu's murder. The event
shook Gikonyo. 'I should have known it was coming,' he told himself,
scared of his own weakness.

Nights followed days with a severe regularity. So Gikonyo started
walking round the compound in the evenings before the sun set. The
walls of each compound into which the camp was divided were
buttressed with barbed-wired; the wall around the whole camp was
covered with barbed-wire. In the morning they went away from the
barbed-wire to the roads and quarries; in the evening they returned
to the barbed-wire. Barbed-wire, barbed-wire everywhere. So it was
today, so it would be tomorrow. The barbed-wire blurred his vision.
There was nothing beyond it. Human voices had stopped. The world,
outside, was dead. No, perhaps, he thought as he went towards the
wall of barbed-wire, it was his ears that had gone dumb, his eyes
blind. For days he went without food, he lived on water, and did not
feel hungry or weak.

He blankly stared into the wire one evening, and with sudden
excitement, wanted to cry or laugh, but did neither. Slowly and
deliberately (he stood outside himself and watched his actions as
from a distance) he pushed his right hand into the wire and pressed
his flesh into the sharp metallic thorns. Gikonyo felt the prick into the
flesh, but not the pain. He withdrew the hand and watched the blood
ooze; he shuddered and enjoyed a strange exhilaration.

The warder held the gun firmly, waiting for Gikonyo to attempt to
break, and seeing that he did not, called him. Gikonyo heard the
voice, a distant echo, and walked towards it, elated by his new
experience. He suddenly stood before the warder, stared insolently
into his face and then raised the hand for the warder to see the blood
and perhaps become envious. The warder (one of the few gentle

ones) saw the glaze in Gikonyo's eyes. 'Go in and rest,' he told him and abruptly turned and walked away, almost running from Gikonyo's weird laughter. In his cell, Gikonyo found that everything – the barbed-wired, Yala Camp, Thabai – was dissolved into a colourless mist. He struggled to recall the outline of Mumbi's face without success, there was only a succession of images each one cancelling out the one immediately preceding it. Was he dead? He put his hand on his chest, felt the heart-beat and knew that he was alive. Why then couldn't he fix a permanent outline of Mumbi in his mind? Perhaps she too had dissolved into the mist. He tried to relive the scene in the wood and was surprised to see he could not experience anything; the desire, the full manhood, the haunting voice of Mumbi, the explosion, no feeling came even as a thing of the past. And all this time, Gikonyo watched himself act – his every gesture, his flow of thought. He was both in and outside himself – in a trance, considering everything calmly, and only mildly puzzled by the failure of his memory. Maybe I'm weary, the thought crossed his mind. If I stand up, everything that makes me what I am will rush back into activity. So he stood up and indeed things seemed to rush back into activity.

The room for instance went round and round – he attempted to walk; panic suddenly seized him, he staggered against the wall, a grunt emitted from his mouth as he slumped back on to the floor, into total darkness.

Wole Soyinka

From *Madmen and Specialists* (1970)

This play was written in response to the atrocities of the Biafran war. Bero is a medical doctor turned torturer. Si Bero is his sister. In his absence she has been learning traditional herbal medicine from two wise old women, Iya Agba and Iya Mate.

Si Bero	They told me what to look for, where to look for it. How to sort them and preserve them.
Bero	[nods] You haven't wasted your time. I still need things from my former vocation.
Si Bero	Former vocation?
Bero	A means, not an end.
Si Bero	We heard terrible things. So much evil. Then I would

	console myself that I earned the balance by carrying on your work. One thing cancels out another. Bero, they're waiting. Go and greet them Bero. They held your life together while you were away.
BERO	What is that supposed to mean?
SI BERO	I never feared for you while they were here.
BERO	You really disappoint me. You are supposed to be intelligent. It was you I asked to do my work, not some stupid old hags. I suppose they filled your head with all that evil stuff. You've been pretty free with that word.
SI BERO	Not you yourself Bero, but guilt contaminates. And often I was afraid … *[Suddenly determined]* Bero, where is Father?
BERO	Safe.
SI BERO	*[stubbornly]* But you must know when he's coming.
BERO	Sometime.
SI BERO	When? Why didn't you return together?
BERO	He's a sick man. He is coming home to be cured.
SI BERO	Sick? Wounded?
BERO	Mind sickness. We must be kind to him.
SI BERO	How long, Bero? How long had he been sick?
BERO	Ever since he came out. Maybe the … suffering around him proved too much for him. His mind broke under the strain.
SI BERO	*[quietly]* How bad? Don't hide anything, Bero. How bad is he?
BERO	He started well. But of course we didn't know which way his mind was working. Madmen have such diabolical cunning. It was fortunate I had already proved myself. He was dangerous. Dangerous!
SI BERO	What do you mean? Did he endanger you?
BERO	Did he! He was in a different sector, working among the convalescents. I wouldn't have known what was going on if I had still been with the Medical Corps.
SI BERO	If you had still been?
BERO	I told you. I switched.
SI BERO	But how? You have your training. How does one switch, just like that?
BERO	You are everything once you go out there. In an emergency … *[He shrugs]* The head of the Intelligence Section died rather suddenly. Natural causes.
SI BERO	And that's the new vocation?
BERO	None other, sister, none other. The Big Braids agreed I

	was born into it. Not that that was any recommendation. They are all submental apes.
SI BERO	*[studying him avidly, a slow apprehension beginning to show on her face]* But you have … you have given that up now. You are back to your real work. Your practice.
BERO	*[turns calmly to meet her gaze]* Practice? Yes, I intend to maintain that side of my practice. A laboratory is important. Everything helps. Control, sister, control. Power comes from bending Nature to your will. The Specialist they called me, and a specialist is – well – a specialist. You analyse, you diagnose, you – *[He aims an imaginary gun]* – prescribe.
SI BERO	*[more to herself]* You should have told me. I have made pledges I cannot fulfil.
BERO	Pledges? What are you talking about?
SI BERO	I swore I was sure of you, only then would they help me.
BERO	Who? The Old Women?
SI BERO	They held nothing back from me.

V.S. Naipaul

From *A Bend in the River* (1979)

The narrator, Salim, who has bought a trading post in the African interior, ponders the nature of the river at night. Big Man is the African dictator who rules the country and who instigates a corrupt and failing modernisation programme. Though the country remains unnamed throughout the novel, this work is based on Naipaul's travels through Central Africa. As such, the novel has historical and literary resonances with Conrad's 'Heart of Darkness' (1902).

Going home at night! It wasn't often that I was on the river at night. I never liked it. I never felt in control. In the darkness of river and forest you could be sure only of what you could see – and even on a moonlight night you couldn't see much. When you made a noise – dipped a paddle in the water – you heard yourself as though you were another person. The river and the forest were like presences, and much more powerful than you. You felt unprotected, an intruder.

In the daylight – though the colours could be very pale and ghostly, with the heat mist at times suggesting a colder climate – you could imagine the town being rebuilt and spreading. You could imagine the forests being uprooted, the roads being laid across creeks and swamps. You could imagine the land being made part of the present: that was how the Big Man put it later, offering us the vision of a two-hundred-mile 'industrial park' along the river. (But he didn't mean it really; it was only his wish to appear a greater magician than any the place had ever known.) In daylight, though, you could believe in that vision of the future. You could imagine the land being made ordinary, fit for men like yourself, as small parts of it had been made ordinary for a short while before independence – the very parts that were now in ruins.

But at night, if you were on the river, it was another thing. You felt the land taking you back to something that was familiar, something you had known at some time but had forgotten or ignored, but which was always there. You felt the land taking you back to what was there a hundred years ago, to what had been there always.

Tsitsi Dangarembga

From *Nervous Conditions* (1988)

Tambudzai, the narrator, a black girl from a poor rural background, has been offered a scholarship to an élite, predominantly white convent. Her cousin, Nyasha, is far more cynical about the opportunity. Babamukuru is her uncle, who would be responsible for paying the extra fees. The novel is set in Rhodesia, now Zimbabwe.

Of course, I did not appreciate the gravity of my situation at that time, my only experience of those people having been with charitable Doris and the fervent missionaries on the mission. But Nyasha knew them and was alarmed. She could not hide, did not even try to hide, her disappointment when I told her how thrilled I was, what an experience I would have, what an opportunity it was, how I intended to put that opportunity to maximum use. She thought there were more evils than advantages to be reaped from such an opportunity. It would be a marvellous opportunity, she said sarcastically, to forget. To forget who you were, what you were and why you were that. The process, she said, was called assimilation, and that was what was intended for the precocious few who might prove a nuisance if left to themselves, whereas the others – well really, who cared about the others? So they made a little space into which you were assimilated, an honorary space in which you could join them and they could make sure that you behaved yourself. I would be comfortable in such a position, she remarked nastily, because look how well I had got on with Babamukuru. But, she insisted, one ought not to occupy that space. Really, one ought to refuse. In my case that meant not going to the nun's mission. 'You'll fall for their tricks,' she said, pointing out that I would obtain a much more useful education at the mission.

If she hadn't said that, that last bit about education at the mission, I might have believed her, but everybody knew that the European schools had better equipment, better teachers, better furniture, better food, better everything. The idea that anything about our mission could be better than theirs was clearly ridiculous. Besides, once you were given a place at one of their schools, you went on and on until you'd finished your 'A' levels. You didn't have to worry about eliminating exams at every stage of the way. That was how it was. That was how it would be. If you were clever, you slipped through any loophole you could find. I for one was going to take any opportunity that came my way. I was quite sure about that; I was very determined. The latest opportunity was this one of going to the convent. I would go. I was sure of myself. I was not sceptical like Nyasha. How could I possibly forget my brother and the mealies, my mother and the latrine and the wedding? These were all evidence of the burdens my mother had succumbed to. Going to the convent was a chance to lighten those burdens by entering a world where burdens were light. I would take the chance. I would lighten my burdens. I would go. If Babamukuru would let me.

Still Nyasha was not impressed. 'Really, Tambudzai,' she said severely when I had finished glorifying my interests, 'there'll always be brothers and mealies and mothers too tired to clean latrines. Whether you go to the convent or not. There's more to be done than that.' This was typical of Nyasha, this obstinate idealism. But she could afford it, being my affluent uncle's daughter. Whereas I, I had to take whatever chances came my way.

Ben Okri

From *The Famished Road* (1991)

The narrator, Azaro, is an *abiku*, a spirit-child, destined to die and be reborn, existing in both the spirit world and earthly reality. His father, having been boxing with a 'Fighting Ghost', has been brought home. Ade, an epileptic and Azoro's companion, is also a spirit-child. The novel is set in modern Nigeria.

The beggars shuffled. The beggar girl got up, touched me on the head, making my flesh bristle, and led the others out of the room. They left silently. Ade lay down on the mat, his eyes swimming. Occasionally he twitched. He had a wan smile on his lips. I leant over him.

'I am going to die soon,' he said.

'Why do you say that?'

'My time has come. My friends are calling me.'

'What friends?'

'In the other world,' he said.

We were silent.

'And what are you two whispering about, eh?' Mum asked.

'Nothing.'

'What happened to him?'

'He's not well.'

'What about his father?'

'I don't know.'

'God save me,' Mum cried.

The candles went out. Mum shut the door and searched for the matches.

'This life! No rest. None. A woman suffers, a woman sweats, with no rest, no happiness. My husband, in three fights. God knows what all this is doing to his brain. This life is too much for me. I am going to hang myself one of these days,' Mum said.

'Don't do that, Mum,' I said.

'Shut up,' she said.

I was silent. Deep in me old songs began to stir. Old voices from the world of spirits. Songs of seductive purity, with music perfect like light and diamonds. Ade twitched. The floor began to shake. I could hear his bones rattling. Mum lit a candle. She sat on Dad's chair, rocking back and forth, her eyes fixed, her face unforgiving. I felt sad. Ade smiled strangely again, sinking deeper into his weird epileptic ecstasy. I leant over him.

'Trouble is always coming. Maybe it's just as well,' he said. 'Your story has just begun. Mine is ending. I want to go to my other home. Your mother is right; there is too much unnecessary suffering on this earth.'

His voice had taken on the timbre of an old man. Soon I recognised it. A snake went up my spine and I couldn't stop shivering. He went on, speaking in the cracked sepulchral voice of the blind old man.

'My time is coming. I have worn out my mother's womb and now she can't have any more children. Coming and going, I have seen the world, I have seen the future. The Koran says nothing is ever finished.'

'What will happen?' I asked him.

Quivering, biting his lips till he drew blood, he said: 'There will be the rebirth of a father. A man with seven heads will take you away. You will come back. You will stay. Before that the spirits and our ancestors will hold a great meeting to discuss the future of the world. It will be one of the most important meetings ever held. Suffering is coming. There will be wars and famine. Terrible things will happen. New diseases, hunger, the rich eating up the earth, people poisoning the sky and the waters, people going mad in the name of history, the clouds will breathe fire, the spirit of things will dry up, laughter will become strange.'

He stopped. There was a long pause. Then he continued, frightening me.

'There will be changes. Coups. Soldiers everywhere. Ugliness. Blindness. And then when people least expect it a great transformation is going to take place in the world. Suffering people will know justice and beauty. A wonderful change is coming from far away and people will realise the great meaning of struggle and hope. There will be peace. Then people will forget. Then it will all start again, getting worse, getting better. Don't fear. You will always have something to struggle for, even if it is beauty or joy.'

He stopped again. And then his fever changed gear, his voice quivered, his eyes were calm.

'Our country is an abiku country. Like the spirit-child, it keeps coming and going. One day it will decide to remain. It will become strong. I won't see it.'

South Africa

Athol Fugard

From *The Coat* (1966)

Developed through improvisational exercises with the Serpent Players, *The Coat* opens with Lavrenti (originally played by Mulligan Mbikwane) addressing the audience directly. At its first performance, the white South African audience were expecting Wole Soyinka's light satire, *The Lion and the Jewel* (1959).

> *Five chairs on an empty stage. The actors – three men and two women – walk on and sit down. One of the men comes forward and addresses the audience.*

LAVRENTI   We are a group of actors from New Brighton. Aniko, Marie, Haemon, Jingi … *[the actors nod as they are introduced]* … and I am Lavrenti.

New Brighton. I often wonder what that name means to outsiders, like you. I am using the word in its purely descriptive sense – we live inside and you live outside. That world where your servants go at the end of the day, that ugly scab of pondokkies and squalor that spoils the approach to Port Elizabeth. If you are interested in knowing something about it we might be able to help you, because we accepted the chance to come here tonight so that we could tell you about a coat, a man's coat, which came back to New Brighton in a stranger's shopping bag.

Allow me a short word of explanation.

There are many confused and even contradictory reasons for our existence as a group. The hunger for applause, boredom, conceit, desperation, even money at one stage – though we have now learnt enough to know that here in Port Elizabeth, Theatre is not the way you make it, but lose it. We have talked about this question of motives more times than I care to remember. But during all that talking we have discovered one thing which we all have in common, something on top of all the other reasons, or should I say at the bottom, because it hasn't been all that strong. We want to use the theatre. For what? Here it gets a bit confused again. Some of us say to understand the world we live in, but we also boast a few idealists who think that Theatre might have something to do with changing it.

These attitudes imply something of a purpose to our work. This in turn has involved us in the life and people of New Brighton. It is the only world we know. It is real. We want our work to be real. So we study and try to understand that world – the shopkeepers and the housewives who complain about the shopkeepers; the labourers coming home tired at night and the bus conductors who don't wait for those labourers at bus stops; the tsotsis who molest the young lovers, the young lovers themselves … as one of us once put it, its problems and its pleasures.

It was in this way that we first heard and talked about the coat.

To begin with, I don't think any of us believed we had anything to learn from it. That was a mistake of course – but remember we are still only beginners, still learning the first lessons and making the first mistakes.

We discovered that the coat was real. I don't mean that we didn't believe it had ever existed. We knew it had. When I say 'real' I mean we discovered that it was the cause and effect of things. We came to believe in it so strongly that we decided to use tonight to show you what had happened when we discussed and examined it. There are certain facts; we will give you them. There are a lot of questions; we tried to find the answers. Listen and judge for yourself.

Nadine Gordimer

From *Burger's Daughter* (1979)

Towards the end of the novel, Rosa Burger, on returning to South Africa from Europe, begins work as a physiotherapist in a black hospital. The setting of this passage is the township of Soweto in 1976.

The children Rosa was teaching to walk who were born crippled were getting excellent rehabilitative care, better than her doctor half-brother could dream about providing in Tanzania. In the second half of 1976 those who were born deformed were joined by those who had been shot. The school riots filled the hospital; the police who answered stones with machine-guns and patrolled Soweto firing revolvers at any street-corner group of people encountered, who raided High Schools and picked off the targets of youngsters escaping in the stampede, also wounded anyone else who happened to be within the random of their fire. The hospital itself was threatened by a counter-surge of furious sorrow that roused the people of Soweto to burn and pillage everything the whites had 'given' in token for all, through three centuries, they had denied the blacks. The million or more (no one knows the exact figure) residents of Soweto have no municipality of their own; a white official who had done what he could, within the white-run welfare system for blacks, to help them endure their lives, was stoned and kicked to death. Other white officials had narrow escapes; several were rescued and hidden safely by blacks themselves, in their own houses. There was no way of identifying one's white face as one that was different from any other, one that should be spared. The white doctors and other personnel among the hospital staff drove back and forth between the hospital and the white city of Johannesburg every day, privileged to pass through police roadblocks that isolated the Soweto area, and at the risk of being surrounded and dragged from their cars as they moved along the road where the armoured police vehicles the people called Hippos had gone before them, raising fists useless against steel plates and guns.

After the funerals of the first wave of children and youths killed by the police, at each successive burial black people were shot while gathered to pay homage to their dead or at the washing of hands at the house of the bereaved that is their custom. The police said it was impossible to distinguish between mourners and the mob; and they spoke more truly than they knew – mourning and anger were fused.

J.M. Coetzee

From *Life and Times of Michael K* (1983)

In the novel's final moments, Michael K, a vagrant simpleton, who has escaped from a detention camp and returned to his former home at Sea Point, meditates upon his 'mistake' and a possible moral. Michael K had lived alone on the farm, until being arrested by government forces. He was to have taken his mother there, to the place of her birth, but she died en route in Stellenbosch.

The mistake I made, he thought, going back in time, was not to have had plenty of seeds, a different packet of seeds for each pocket: pumpkin seeds, marrow seeds, beans, carrot seeds, beetroot seeds, onion seeds, tomato seeds, spinach seeds. Seeds in my shoes too, and in the lining of my coat, in case of robbers along the way. Then my mistake was to plant all my seeds together in one patch. I should have planted them one at a time spread out over miles of veld in patches of soil no larger than my hand, and drawn a map and kept it with me at all times so that every night I could make a tour of the sites to water them. Because if there was one thing I discovered out in the country, it was that there is time enough for everything.

(Is that the moral of it all, he thought, the moral of the whole story: that there is time enough for everything? Is that how morals come, unbidden, in the course of events, when you least expect them?)

He thought of the farm, the grey thornbushes, the rocky soil, the ring of hills, the mountains purple and pink in the distance, the great still blue empty sky, the earth grey and brown beneath the sun save here and there, where if you looked carefully you suddenly saw a tip of vivid green, pumpkin leaf or carrot-brush.

It did not seem impossible that whoever it was who disregarded the curfew and came when it suited him to sleep in this smelly corner (K imagined him as a little old man with a stoop and a bottle in his side pocket who muttered all the time into his beard, the kind of old man the police ignored) might be tired of life at the seaside and want to take a holiday in the country if he could find a guide who knew the roads. They could share a bed tonight, it had been done before; in the morning, at first light, they could go out searching the back streets for an abandoned barrow; and if they were lucky the two of them could be spinning along the high road by ten o'clock, remembering to stop on the way to buy seeds and one or two other things, avoiding Stellenbosch perhaps, which seemed to be a place of ill luck.

And if the old man climbed out of the cart and stretched himself (things were gathering pace now) and looked at where the pump had been that the soldiers had blown up so that nothing should be left standing, and complained, saying, 'What are we going to do about water?,' he, Michael K, would produce a teaspoon from his pocket, a teaspoon and a long roll of string. He would clear the rubble from the mouth of the shaft, he would bend the handle of the teaspoon in a loop and tie the string to it, he would lower it down the shaft deep into the earth, and when he brought it up there would be water in the bowl of the spoon; and in that way, he would say, one can live.

The Caribbean

C.L.R. James

From *Minty Alley* (1936)

At this point in James' novel about 'barrack-yard' life, the young intellectual is confided in by Mrs. Rouse. Mr. Benoit, her lover, has been unfaithful to her. Maisie is her niece and Philomen an Indian servant.

She held her head back and it quivered on her neck. Indignation, justifiable, shone in her eyes and transfigured her face. Over the lips towered the Roman nose. She spoke with power.

'God will punish him, Mr. Haynes. He can't escape. I am going to see him suffer. I am going to see Mr. Benoit suffer. You can see the wrong he have done me. I can see it. Everybody can see it. You don't think God can see it, too? He watching, He seeing, He saying nothing, but He not sleeping. God don't like ugly, Mr. Haynes, and tears of blood going to run from Mr. Benoit's eyes for the misery he have caused me. His heart hurting him where he is. If things was going nice and easy it would hurt him, much less now that he seeing trouble. His mind going to come back to me. As I tell him one day when we was quarrelling about the woman, he say he was going. I tell him, "Go, but you will never forget me."

> '"Where every you may be, by land or by sea
> My spirit before you, you will ever see."

'Mr. Haynes, I have been more than a wife to him. I have been a mother. I nurse him in sickness. I shield him from harm. And he gone and leave me. But let him go with that woman. The day will come when he will call for the one he leave behind.

'Mr. Haynes, if my little child that died was alive today so that I could hold her to my bosom and cherish her, or if Maisie was a different child, a girl who could comfort me, it wouldn't be so hard. What hurts me is that I have nobody.

'But, Mr. Haynes,' her voice which had softened rose again, 'Maisie not going to stay in my house after I put my business in order. I can't keep her here. She brings back all my wrongs when I see her. You see I leave her alone. I don't ask her to do anything. I leave her to do what she want. All the work I have I fight with it, me and Philomen. She knew everything, Mr. Haynes, and she used to be standing by the gate on a Sunday morning looking to see when I coming up while the two of them carrying on inside. The girl betray my honour for vanilla ice-cream and sugar cake. And the man didn't have no shame. Look who he had assisting him in his nastiness. A child who used to call him Pappy, and who he held in his arms as a baby. I well rid of him. Yes, Mr. Haynes, I well rid of him. Men change. They all right in prosperity, but when adversity come, then you see the bones of them. You are a gentleman, Mr. Haynes, and I can tell you this. If you know what Mr. Benoit ask me to do a few months before you come to live here! Races was coming on and he wanted a suit and money to go. He tell me to go to town and see Mr. Nesfield who carry on that grocery in Main Street. We used to deal there long ago. He tell me to go and tell Mr. Nesfield we in difficulty and if he could lend us fifty dollars. I tell him: "McCarthy, try and do without the money. Let us keep down a little and then we will have times as before." Mr. Haynes, the man make such a row that for peace I had to go. And when I dress the morning to go he call me and tell me: "A, you know if Mr. Nesfield scrupling to lend you the money and he offer to you, that wouldn't be nothing if you take him. As long as you don't do it in secret behind my back i's all right." That what he tell me, Mr. Haynes. After we live sixteen years and I was a true and faithful – I was true and faithful. You don't see the man didn't have any respect for me? I was only his convenience.'

V.S. Reid

From *New Day* (1949)

The novel's narrator, Joseph Campbell, relates how his brother, Davie, gave evidence to a Royal Commision sent to investigate the Morant Bay Uprising, Jamaica in 1865. *New Day* was the first Caribbean novel to use Creole as its main narrative medium.

"Man was no' built for slavery, Your Honours. In him are the Image and Likeness, and it is no' of the skin. Inside o' him there is the dignity of God, whether he was birthed in a hut or in a buckra's mansion. And that dignity o' God tells him say he should no' a serf to another. But for two hundred years on this island, men ha' been serfs to the buckra planter.

"They did no' take it quietly. Often much blood flowed. For although they read no books of history what could tell them of the road followed by the bonded before them, yet the dignity inside every born man would 'low no rest to these slaves. There was something else too.

"For these two hundred years they saw the shaming of man's highest calling – the calling o' labour with the hands, the sweat by which the Big Master said we should eat our bread. The shaming o' labour? Make me tell you of this, Your Honours."

The Commissioners have no' made any moves, but you can sense say they are saying that Davie should tell them of the shaming. My bro' will …

"Howsoever, Emancipation came in 'Thirty-eight, and the buckra said they were free and gave them some acres of rock and cactus."

My bro' took a breath. His voice came easy again.

"What happened when this freedom came? What happened when buckra said he would now pay them wages for their work? Did they take tasks in the fields for money where not long ago they took it for the lash?

"Ask the government in Kingston-town. You will hear that never was the cane crop so poor as after the Emancipation; that estates after estates pawned their titles. Hand labour did no' have beauty to men longer, for they did no' like the scent of sugar-cane longer. Stir the soft earth 'tween the rocks and the cactus, and enough-plenty yams would be grown for their own bellies. Then they work from day-cloud to evening star longer?"

Heads of the Commissioners on the Bench nodded to each other as my bro' took breath and pushed his hair from his forehead. Now he talks straight at the Commissioners, leaning forward on the rail.

"Aie, Your Honours, it is no' whether one was right or wrong, but I am telling of the case for they who marched on Morant Bay court-house. I say there would ha' been no march if buckra had made it well for them to stay home."

Una Marson

'Kinky Hair Blues' (1937)

The persona of this Creole poem bemoans the desire of Jamaican men for white-looking women.

Gwine find a beauty shop
Cause I ain't a belle.
Gwine find a beauty shop
Cause I ain't a lovely belle.
The boys pass me by,
The say I's not swell.

See oder young gals
So slick and smart.
See dose oder young gals
So slick and smart.
I jes gwine die on de shelf
If I don't mek a start.

I hate dat ironed hair
And dat bleaching skin.
Hate dat ironed hair
And dat bleaching skin.
But I'll be all alone
If I don't fall in.

Lord,'tis you did gie me
All dis kinky hair
'Tis you did gie me
All dis kinky hair,
And I don't envy gals
What got dose locks so fair.

I like me black face
And me kinky hair.
I like me black face
And me kinky hair.
But nobody loves dem,
I jes don't tink it's fair.

Now I's gwine press me hair
And bleach me skin.
I's gwine press me hair
And bleach me skin.
What won't a gal do
Some kind of man to win.

Louise Bennett

From 'Jamaica Oman' (1983)

Below are the first nine stanzas of this Creole poem, which is rich in Jamaican
vocabulary and reference: 'cunny' is smart or crafty; 'jinnal' is a trickster; 'Maroon
Nanny' is a national hero – she is said to have led escaped slaves (Maroons) in war
against the British and had the ability to catch bullets in her buttocks before
sending them back to the British; 'pickney' means 'child'; Spellin-Bee is an
American spelling competition entered by Jamaican school children; 'so-so rib'
means 'little rib' and is a reference to God taking one of Adam's ribs to create Eve;
'tallawah' is sturdy.

Jamaica oman, cunny, sah!
Is how dem jinnal so?
Look how long dem liberated
An de man dem never know!

Look how long Jamaica oman
– Modder, sister, wife, sweetheart –
Outer road an eena yard deh pon
A dominate her part!

From Maroon Nanny teck her body
Bounce bullet back pon man,
To when nowadays gal-pickney tun
Spellin-Bee champion.

From de grass root to de hill-top,
In profession, skill an trade,
Jamaica oman teck her time
Dah mount an meck de grade.

Some backa man a push, some side-a
Man a hole him han,
Some a lick sense eena man head,
Some a guide him pon him plan!

Neck an neck an foot an foot wid man
She buckle hole her own;
While man a call her 'so-so rib'
Oman a tun backbone!

An long before Oman Lib bruck out
Over foreign lan
Jamaica female wasa work
Her liberated plan!

Jamaica oman know she strong,
She know she tallawah,
But she no want here pickney-dem
Fi start call her 'Puppa'.

So de cunny Jamma oman
Gwan like pants-suit is a style,
An Jamaica man no know she wear
De trousiz all de while!

V.S. Naipaul

From *Miguel Street* (1959)

Set in Port of Spain, Trinidad, *Miguel Street* is a semi-autobiographical novel about
Naipaul's childhood home. Here, the child narrator marvels at Laura, whose 'eight
children' had 'seven fathers'.

I suppose Laura holds a world record.
  Laura had eight children.
  There is nothing surprising in that.
  These eight children had seven fathers.
  Beat that!
  It was Laura who gave me my first lesson in biology. She lived just
next door to us, and I found myself observing her closely.
  I would notice her belly rising for months.

Then I would miss her for a short time.

And the next time I saw her she would be quite flat.

And the leavening process would begin again in a few months.

To me this was one of the wonders of the world in which I lived, and I always observed Laura. She herself was quite gay about what was happening to her. She used to point to it, and say, 'This thing happening again, but you get use to it after the first three four times. Is a damn nuisance, though.'

She used to blame God, and speak about the wickedness of men.

For her first six children she tried six different men.

Hat used to say, 'Some people hard to please.'

But I don't want to give you the impression that Laura spent all her time having babies and decrying men, and generally feeling sorry for herself. If Bogart was the most bored person in the street, Laura was the most vivacious. She was always gay, and she liked me.

She would give me plums and mangoes when she had them; and whenever she made sugar-cakes she would give me some.

Even my mother, who had a great dislike of laughter, especially in me, even my mother used to laugh at Laura.

She often said to me, 'I don't know why Laura muching you up so for. Like she ain't have enough children to mind.'

I think my mother was right. I don't think a woman like Laura could have ever had too many children. She loved all her children, though you wouldn't have believed it from the language she used when she spoke to them. Some of Laura's shouts and curses were the richest things I have ever heard, and I shall never forget them.

Hat said once, 'Man, she like Shakespeare when it come to using words.'

Laura used to shout, 'Alwyn, you broad-mouth brute, come here.'

And, 'Gavin, if you don't come here this minute, I make you fart fire, you hear.'

And, 'Lorna, you black bow-leg bitch, why you can't look what you doing?'

Derek Walcott

From Part IV of 'A Simple Flame' (1973)

The poet persona recollects meeting Anna, his love, whose house he has approached by rowing boat. The comparison at the end of the poem is Biblical:

Holofernes was a general who had taken over the land of Judah; Judith, who had been brought to him when he was drunk, decapitated him.

And all bread savoured
of her sunburnt nape,

her laughter a white napkin
shaken under the leaves.
We sit by the stone wall

all changes to grey stone,
stone hands, stone air,
stone eyes, from which

irisless, we stare,
wishing the sea were stone,
motion we could not hear.

No silence, since,
its equal.

For one late afternoon, when again she stood
in the door of a twilight always left ajar,
when dusk had softened the first bulb
the colour of the first weak star,
I asked her, 'Choose,'
the amazed dusk held its breath,
the earth's pulse staggered,
she nodded, and that nod
married earth with lightning.

And now we were the first guests of the earth
and everything stood still for us to name.
Against the blades of palms and yellow sand,
I hear that open laugh,
I see her stride
as ruthless as that flax-bright harvester
Judith, with Holofernes' lantern in her hand.

Kamau Brathwaite

From 'Wings of a Dove' (1973)

This is a section from *Rights of Passage*, the opening book of *The Arrivants: A New World Trilogy*. Brother Man, who is introduced here and takes on the voice of the poem, is a Jamaican Rastafarian. 'Babylon' is the Rastafarian term for the corrupt, oppressive world that Rastafarians believe they will be delivered from when they return to Ethiopia, Africa. Babylon was a place of slavery for the Jews of the Old Testament.

Brother Man the Rasta
man, beard full of lichen
brain full of lice
watched the mice
come up through the floor-
boards of his down-
town, shanty-town kitchen,
and smiled. Blessed are the poor
in health, he mumbled,
that they should inherit this
wealth. Blessed are the meek
hearted, he grumbled,
for theirs is this stealth.

Brother Man the Rasta
man, hair full of lichen
head hot as ice
watched the mice
walk into his poor
hole, reached for his peace and the pipe of his ganja
and smiled how the mice
eyes, hot pumice
pieces, glowed into his room
like ruby, like rhinestone
and suddenly startled like
diamond

And I
Rastafar-I
in Babylon's boom
town, crazed by the moon
and the peace of this chalice, I

prophet and singer, scourge
of the gutter, guardian
Trench Town, the Dungle and Young's
Town, rise and walk through the now silent
streets of affliction, hawk's eyes
hard with fear, with
affection, and hear my people
cry, my people
shout:

Down down
white
man con
man brown
man down
down full
man, frown-
ing fat
man that
white black
man that
lives in
the town

Rise rise
locks-
man, Solo-
man wise
man, rise
rise rise
leh we
laugh
dem mock
dem stop
dem kill
dem an' go
back back
to the black
man lan'
back back
to Af-
rica

4 | Critical approaches

- What is post-colonial criticism?

- What are the key critical concepts for discussing colonial and post-colonial texts?

- How might different critical approaches affect your reading of and writing about colonial and post-colonial literature?

The main purpose of this part of the book is to provide an introduction to writing about colonial and post-colonial literature, and to create an awareness of the major issues which have confronted post-colonial critics and authors regarding the discussion of literary texts.

In some ways, the issues which need to be borne in mind when writing about post-colonial literature are a reflection of the changing values of a post-colonial world: criticism of the cultural assumptions of the 'centre', the metropolis, the need to see texts within their cultural contexts and an awareness of the importance of recognising different, perhaps conflicting, readings of the same text. Just as post-colonial literature can be said to challenge dominant forms and expectations, so post-colonial criticism often challenges either established judgements about classic texts from the English canon, or reflects the shifts in focus that began with the break-up of empire.

Part of this process has been the development of new concepts and vocabulary with which to discuss critical ideas and perspectives. Finding and developing an effective critical vocabulary is an important part of writing about post-colonial literature; the reader is encouraged to think about which terms might be most useful or appropriate, as well as which concepts might be most helpful.

The influence of theory on post-colonial criticism

Much of the terminology and thinking behind post-colonial criticism has been shaped by the development of literary theory, particularly in American and European universities. Theorists question basic assumptions about how literature is produced, read, discussed and written about.

One key feature of theory is the use of concepts which have not traditionally been seen as part of 'literary' studies. Literary theorists have utilised work from the fields of linguistics, psychoanalysis and the social sciences in order to open up, dismantle and discuss texts in new ways. Importantly, theorists have been concerned with the ways in which class, race and gender are constructed through language and the ways in which literature supports (or subverts) the dominant values of the society in which it is written. Theorists such as Roland Barthes (1915–1980) and Jacques Derrida have promoted a sceptical approach to reading which questions the authority and role of the author, and even the ability of language to communicate meaning.

It is no coincidence that such developments have gained influence as post-colonial writing has become more prominent. By its very nature, post-colonial writing raises issues of representation, cultural value and the capacity of language to convey meaning or reflect experience. The development of a broad school of post-colonial theory (see Part 5, page 121) is testament to the influence of literary theory in general.

Post-modernist thinking and post-colonial literature

It is also important to bear in mind that much, though certainly not all, discussion of post-colonial literature takes place within the context of post-modernism. Briefly stated, post-modernism seeks to describe late 20th-century art and culture. Post-modernists point to a world which is dominated by mass media, information technology and one which is driven by production and consumption on a global scale. Thus, a novel concerning women in pre-independence Rhodesia becomes a commodity consumed by readers in Europe. A post-modernist might point to the irony of a novel which exposes the injustices of colonialism, yet which serves the readership tastes of the First World.

Post-modernists also highlight a lack of cultural authenticity and purity; instead, they emphasise **pastiche** and hybridity (see page 124). Post-modernism has been criticised for being the intellectual toy of the First World, for promoting political cynicism and for minimising the importance of post-colonial literature's Third World context. However, post-modernists might argue that, by emphasising what is marginal, different and ambiguous, they celebrate post-colonial writers and writing in a way which is unsentimental and reflects the complexity of the contemporary world.

po-mo
hybridity

Key concepts in post-colonial criticism

The concepts introduced here – **discourse, 'Other', hegemony,** hybridity and **difference** – have become particularly important in the discussion of colonial and post-colonial writing. Their real significance lies in the extent to which they can help the reader analyse and understand the texts themselves, and the extent to which they provide a vocabulary with which to discuss relevant ideas.

The material presented here is highly selective. The issue of how to discuss post-colonial literature is itself a complex and, at times controversial, one. The purpose of this section is not to examine the intricacies of that debate, but to provide material which will be useful and allow the reader to come to his/her own judgements about the ideas and vocabulary outlined below.

Discourse

The concept of discourse may, at first, seem vast and intangible, but it has become a key concept in analysing colonial and post-colonial texts. The first major work, in this subject, to be based on the concept was Edward Said's *Orientalism* (1976). In it, Said analysed how the Orient (the Middle and Far East) became an object of European writing and politics, and how the discipline which developed (Orientalism) was an integral part of colonial expansion and rule in the area. In his own words, Orientalism was

Orientalism

> ... the enormously systematic discipline by which European culture was able to manage – and even produce – the Orient politically, sociologically, militarily, ideologically, scientifically and imaginatively ... Moreover, so authoritative a position did Orientalism have that I believe no-one writing, thinking, or acting on the Orient could do so without taking account of the limitations on thought and action imposed by Orientalism.

Two important aspects of discourse can be developed from these statements. First, the culture of empire, in its diverse areas, was an integral part of establishing and maintaining colonial control. Colonial writing and study, even if unwittingly at times, confirmed and supported the enterprise of empire. Secondly, what creates a discourse is the set of rules ('limitations on thought and action') which determine who can speak and what statement will be regarded as valid and what will seem implausible. In this sense, the subject itself determines what can be said about it.

In short, no field of enquiry (whether history, literature or science) is ever completely neutral, but is shaped by the institutions which support it. In a colonial context this is particularly relevant because 'knowledge' about colonised peoples was entwined with a sense of authority over them and this, in turn, justified the need for their control.

A sense of knowledge and authority is also entwined with the issue of how colonised lands and peoples were represented in texts as varied as novels and government reports. Such representations, it can be argued, were 'constructs' in the sense that they were based on ideas and perceptions which had little to do with a genuine understanding of the world being described. The subject is 'produced', and not reflected, through such writing or study. On one level, to analyse colonial discourse is to study how colonised peoples were constructed, represented, even 'silenced' within colonial writing. They were silenced in the sense that their 'voices' were either absent or presented in such a way as to make them worthless or simply a confirmation of negative stereotypes.

The following extract is taken from H.M. Stanley's *In Darkest Africa* (1890). The natives have tried to prevent Stanley crossing a river and entering their village:

> Loads were at once dropped ... and a smart scene of battle-play occurred, at the end of which the natives retreated on the full run. To punish them for four hours persecution of us we turned about and set fire to every hut on either bank ... It should be observed that up to the moment of the firing of the villages the fury of the natives seemed to be increasing, but the instant the flames were devouring their homes the fury ceased, by which we learned that fire had a remarkable sedative influence on their nerves.

▶ In what ways does the language of this passage 'silence' the reality of the natives' experience and even 'exclude' them from being worthy of consideration? How is the language of 'knowledgeable', 'scientific' enquiry used to justify his actions?

In the light of this passage and its assumptions, reflect on why post-colonial writers have been so concerned with issues of representation and about representing their own cultures.

The following lines are by the critic, Michael Gorra, who uses the concept of 'Africanist' discourse in discussing Conrad's classic colonial text, 'Heart of Darkness'.

▶ First, reread the extract from 'Heart of Darkness' (Part 3, pages 70–71) and form your own judgements about Conrad's depiction of Africa and Africans.

- How do you respond to the passage as a modern reader?
- How do you think Conrad's contemporary readers might have responded to it?

Now consider Gorra's analysis:

> Such a discourse even takes the darkness of African skin as the absence of light, a sign that there is something missing, an emptiness that is to be "written on by others," that can be filled with wonder or with horror, with anything but the specificities of actual African lives.
> What is most often written on that slate is the related discourse of primitivism: the return to one's origins, to the earliest state of the world, a world that allows the West to escape from and yet simultaneously underscore its own modernity. The paradigmatic text [writing which exemplifies a particular way of thinking] is of course

'Heart of Darkness', in which Africa becomes a metaphor for man's original state even as it also provides a metaphor for the darkness of the human heart. What Miller [Christopher L. Miller, another critic] demonstrates is the degree to which such literary appropriations become entangled with the history of colonial exploitation ... And Africa itself, as the critical commonplace now holds, becomes identified with evil; so in using the continent as a symbol for European depravity, Conrad's story participates, on the level of language, with the imperialism it appears to condemn.

(from *After Empire*, 1997)

The above criticism is an excellent example of how the concept of discourse can be used when responding to a text and how it affects the way the text itself is read. Rather than seeing 'Heart of Darkness' as an isolated piece of writing, the critic places it in the context of 'Africanist' and then 'primitivist' discourse, so that the reader becomes aware that the text is not a straightforward reflection of Africa, but actually part of the process by which Africa is constructed and invented in the European imagination ('an emptiness that is to be "written on by others"'). Note how the critic sees the text not in terms of the writer's individual experience, but as part of an historical process ('entangled with the history of colonial exploitation'), so that the text's integrity is itself brought into question ('participates, on the level of language, with the imperialism it appears to condemn'). This has the effect of questioning the validity of Conrad's depiction which contains 'anything but the specificities of actual African lives' and is 'a metaphor for the darkness of the human heart'. The question which is raised is: has Conrad created Africa according to his own, European image of it?

▶ Reflect on how the concept of discourse might affect your own reading of the extract from 'Heart of Darkness'. How does it affect your appreciation of the passage 'on the level of language'? To what extent does it make you question how Africa and Africans are depicted? Could one argue that the passage from Achebe's *Things Fall Apart* (Part 3, pages 78–79) attempts to redress the balance by providing us not with a 'metaphor', but with 'the specificities of actual African lives'?

'Other'

The concept of 'Other' is central to thinking about colonial and post-colonial writing. For Said, Orientalist discourse was characterised by a positioning of colonised peoples and places as Other, in the sense of alien, non-Western and, therefore, inferior. In his own words:

> The Orient is not only adjacent to Europe; it is also the place of Europe's greatest, richest and oldest colonies, the source of its civilisations and languages ... and one of its deepest and most recurrent images of the Other ...

▶ The following lines are taken from *Modern Egypt* by Lord Cromer, who was England's representative in Egypt between 1882 and 1907. They are cited in *Orientalism*. How is a sense of Other created in this extract?

> The European is a close reasoner; his statements of fact are devoid of any ambiguity; he is a natural logician, albeit he may not have studied logic; he is by nature sceptical and requires proof before he can accept the truth of any proposition; his trained intelligence works like a piece of mechanism. The mind of the Oriental, on the other hand, like his picturesque streets, is eminently wanting in symmetry. His reasoning is of the most slipshod description ... They are often incapable of drawing the most obvious conclusions from any simple premises of which they admit the truth. Endeavor to elicit a plain statement of facts from an ordinary Egyptian. His explanation will generally be lengthy, and wanting in lucidity. He will probably contradict himself half-a-dozen times before he has finished his story. He will often break down under the mildest process of cross-examination.

▶ Consider briefly how useful you might find the concept of Other for approaching colonial and post-colonial texts.

Hegemony

This concept was first developed by the Italian Marxist, Antonio Gramsci (1981–1937). In *An Introduction to Post-colonial Theory*, by Peter Childs and R.J. Patrick Williams, it has been defined as:

> Gramsci's term for the force by which people are convinced of the naturalness or rightness of their position and that of their rulers ... The political leadership of a hegemonic [dominating] group is through the consent and acceptance of the ruled ... Culture is the site on which the struggle for hegemonic power is conducted.

Clearly, hegemony can be seen as a model for understanding how dominant cultural concepts of the coloniser become imbued by the colonised and how colonial power becomes accepted. Importantly, hegemony helps to explain the collusion of colonised groups and their acceptance of colonial ideology (the beliefs and values which reflect and support the colonial system). Coercing, but voluntary, institutions such as schools or areas of employment play a large part in establishing hegemonic power.

Many post-colonial writers have been interested in both the psychological and cultural effects of colonialism and how its dominant values were internalised by colonial subjects.

▶ Read the extracts from M.R. Anand's *Coolie* and R.K. Narayan's *The English Teacher* (Part 3, pages 71–73 and pages 74–75). In what ways is British hegemony in India represented in these passages? What indication is there of resistance to it?

Hybridity

If empire was supported by concepts which divided the world strictly into neat categories (coloniser/colonised, civilised/savage, Western/Eastern, European/African), then the post-colonial world is perhaps characterised by a breakdown of such strict definitions. This sense of mixing or hybridity is reflected on both cultural and literary levels.

Rather than seeing texts as part of a dominant or resistant culture, critics who emphasise hybridity also emphasise the eclectic nature of post-colonial writing, in terms of both style and content. They celebrate writers' ability to utilise whatever traditions are available to them. For instance, Salman Rushdie openly acknowledges literary influences which range from Indian myths and oral storytelling techniques to European experimental writers such as the German novelist Günter Grass. It is perhaps most important to realise that through such mixing, new hybrid forms are emerging.

The concept of hybridity, as opposed to that of cultural purity, has a very material relevance. Coca Cola is drunk in India and traditional Indian music influences records produced in America. With the development of travel, global communication and global markets, the post-colonial world has become a world of entwined but distinctive elements. Not only are authors themselves aware of a range of international influences, but the reality which they reflect is increasingly shaped by the breakdown of previously distinct cultural boundaries. The following passage is from Arundhati Roy's *The God of Small Things*. This extract is set in a hotel that was once a colonial residence in Kerala, a province of India:

> The Hotel People liked to tell their guests that the oldest of the
> wooden houses, with its air-tight, panelled storeroom which could
> hold enough rice to feed an army for a year, had been the ancestral

home of Comrade E.M.S. Namboodiripad, 'Kerala's Mao Tse-Tung,' they explained to the uninitiated. The furniture and knicknacks that came with the house were on display. A reed umbrella, a wicker couch, a wooden Dowry Box. They were labelled with edifying placards which said Traditional Kerala Umbrella and Traditional Bridal Dowry Box.

So there it was, History and Literature enlisted by commerce. Kurtz and Karl Marx joining hands to greet rich guests as they stepped off the boat ...

In the evenings (for that regional flavour) the tourists were treated to truncated kathakali performances ('Small attention spans,' the Hotel People explained to the dancers). So ancient stories were collapsed and amputated. Six-hour classics were slashed to twenty-minute cameos.

▶ Which aspects of this passage might be considered hybrid? What might the author be saying about the nature of indigenous culture in a modern, consumer society?

Difference

If 'hybridity' is one extreme of post-colonialism, then cultural distinctiveness is the other. Asserting 'difference' from the colonial centre can be done in a number of ways, such as using non-English vocabulary, depicting specific cultural practices or alluding to indigenous literature or oral traditions. On one level, it acts as a way of asserting a specific culture in opposition to the stereotypes which made up a picture of empire.

The effect can be to create a 'distance' between the text and the reader who is not familiar with what is depicted or the vocabulary used. This distance, it can be argued, is significant because of the uncertainty and ambiguity it creates. Such gaps in understanding reflect those aspects of different cultures which are, at least immediately, unbridgeable.

also points to experience of 'universal' texts by others

▶ Consider how relevant the ideas of difference and distance have been to your reading of post-colonial literature so far.

The critics Bill Ashcroft, Gareth Griffiths and Helen Tiffin highlight this when commenting on a passage from Ngugi's *A Grain Of Wheat*. They are commenting on Ngugi's use of **allusion:**

Allusion and Difference

Allusion can perform the same function of registering cultural distance in the post-colonial text ... An example of this is Ngugi wa

Thiong'o's novel *A Grain of Wheat* in which Gikonyo sings the following song to his future wife Mumbi:

'Haven't you heard the new song?'
    'Which? Sing it.'
    'You know it too. I believe it is Kihika who introduced it here. I only remember the words of the chorus:

    Gikuyu na Mumbi
    Gikuyu na Mumbi
    Gikuyu na Mumbi
    Nikihui ngwatiro.'

It was Mumbi who now broke the solemnity. She was laughing quietly.
    'What is it?
    'Oh, Carpenter, Carpenter. So you know why I came?'
    'I don't!' he said, puzzled.
    'But you sing to *me* and *Gikuyu* telling us it is burnt at the *handle*.'
                                                        (Ngugi, 1967)

This simple chorus is dense with **cultural signifiers** [in this case, words which act as signs, both within and about the culture to which they belong]. Gikuyu was the first man of the Kikuyu tribe, the man from whom all Kikuyu were descended, and Mumbi was his wife, the first woman. 'Nikihui' literally means something that is ready and cooked. 'Ngwatiro' is literally a handle. But when used together the term means that someone is in trouble because the handle is too hot. The song as invented by Kihika means that the relationship between a man and a woman spells trouble. The relationship is too hot to handle and as a chorus it has both sexual and political overtones. But Mumbi laughs because it foretells her reason for visiting Gikonyo: her panga handle has actually been burnt in the fire and needs repair.

This example confirms the absence which lies at the point of interface between two cultures. Here it is demonstrated by Ngugi's refusal to gloss (translate) the song directly and the consequent exchange between the man and the woman. This does not mean that the song cannot be understood once the whole context is grasped, but rather that the process of allusion installs linguistic distance itself as the subject of the text.

(From *The Empire Writes Back*, 1989)

▶ How do you respond to this analysis? To what extent does it aid your appreciation of the extract they have quoted?

Consider the use of technical vocabulary. Does it hinder or aid communication? What kind of reader was their analysis written for? What assumptions do they have about him or her? Which readers would not experience 'linguistic distance' from the text?

▶ Reread the lines from Ngugi and form your own response to it. What kinds of specialist vocabulary might you use if you were to communicate your response in writing?

Feminist criticism

If post-colonial criticism invites a reappraisal of colonial texts and develops a vocabulary for discussing post-colonial literature, then **feminist** criticism extends that process to include an analysis of how women are represented in colonial and post-colonial literature. The purpose behind this is to challenge assumptions and stereotypes about women in both literature and society. Indeed, male writing can be seen as reflecting the values of the patriarchal society to which it belongs.

Feminist literary criticism has a particular relevance in a post-colonial context. Though both colonialism and patriarchy have been closely entwined historically, an end to formal empire has not meant an end to the oppression of women in the former colonies. On a literary level, post-colonial feminists point to the ways in which women continue to be stereotyped and marginalised, ironically by post-colonial authors who might themselves claim to be challenging a culture of oppression.

▶ To develop this important aspect of feminist criticism, read the extract taken from Derek Walcott's long, meditative poem 'A Simple Flame', published in *Another Life*, (Part 3, pages 98–99).

Make a note of your initial thoughts and feelings:

- How would you describe the form and tone of the poem?

- What experiences are conveyed in the poem?

- What is the relationship between the persona of the poem and Anna?

- How is Anna depicted?

Now consider the following response from the feminist critic, Elaine Savory Fido, from her essay 'Macho Attitudes and Derek Walcott' (in *Literature In The Modern World*, 1990), in which she analyses Walcott's representation of Anna as a female character:

> Fortunately, given his attitudes to women, Walcott's creative world is a predominantly male one, in which men have close and important understanding of each other. He also deals with racism, colonialism

and the situation of the poor masses with intelligence, anger and originality. But his treatment of women is full of clichés, stereotypes and negativity ...

In the portrait of Anna, youthful love of the poet-persona in *Another Life,* there is a threatening quality which Edward Baugh has considered:

> I see her stride
> as ruthless as that flax-bright harvester
> Judith, with Holofernes' lantern in her hand.

(This too is a kind of idealisation, as Judith by her murder of Holerfernes, proved herself a partner and heroine; but the connotations which adhere to her when she is seen from Holofernes' point of view are inescapable, complicating Anna's connotations of simplicity and truth.

[from Edward Baugh *Derek Walcott: Memory as Vision,* 1978])

This image of Anna as a murderous female (perceived via the masonry of maleness rather than through the role she plays in her culture by her action) comes after a description of sexual energy in a mildly threatening context:

> For one late afternoon, when again she stood
> in the door of a twilight always left ajar,
> when dusk had softened the first bulb
> the colour of the first weak star,
> I asked her, Choose,
> the amazed dusk held its breath,
> the earth's pulse staggered,
> she nodded, and that nod
> married earth with lightning ...
>
> I see that open laugh,
> I see her stride ...

The images of Anna here are idealised, romanticised ... but there is a sense of the energy of this young woman being part of natural forces which could be hostile to the poet. The fear of strong female sexuality which characterises patriarchy is present here: Anna is young and innocent but there is that about her which will be powerful, and it is this quality which creates conflict in the poet-persona.

▶ When responding to another's views, it is essential to test their ideas against the text itself. How fair do you find Elaine Savory Fido's critique of Walcott's portrayal of Anna? Is the image of Anna 'idealised, romanticised'? Is there a 'fear of strong female sexuality' present in the poem?

Consider briefly the language used by the critic to express her views. Which phrases did you find particularly effective? Note how Elaine Savory Fido referred to another critic, Edward Baugh: how did this strengthen or clarify her argument?

▶ What you would have chosen to highlight in a commentary on the sections of the poem discussed? What evidence you would have used to support your own ideas?

How to write about post-colonial literature

As may already be clear, writing about post-colonial literature is far from uniform and can reflect a variety of different critical approaches and ideas. Any 'how to' section is bound to have limitations, and for an important reason: writing about post-colonial literature should be an individual process, with your own response to the text at the centre.

This does not exclude considering other people's writings or seeing a text in context. In fact, these are often essential and creative ways of coming to an individual appreciation. However, cultivating an individual approach does emphasise the importance of the works themselves and your engagement with what the authors have produced.

At this point, it is important to emphasise how entwined reading and writing about post-colonial literature are. Indeed, criticism is often said to present a 'reading' of a text. When writing about post-colonial literature it is essential not to exclude the issues discussed in Part 2: Approaching the texts. Concepts such as hybridity and difference can be seen in terms of the use of indigenous and colonising traditions or the appropriation of English, to name only two significant areas. Sensitive, detailed reading must be at the centre of writing about post-colonial literature.

Using critical concepts and vocabulary

An important point first: critical vocabulary is only a tool, designed to enhance the discussion of texts, and not an end in itself. As with any tool, it is important to use it appropriately. The use of critical vocabulary should not be seen as a substitute for understanding, but as a way of communicating ideas precisely and economically.

The key concepts of post-colonial criticism can also be seen as tools in that they can provide effective frameworks for analysing texts and distinguishing between different kinds of post-colonial writing. An important aspect of learning to write about post-colonial literature is learning how to use such concepts and vocabulary effectively. The following tasks are designed to support that process.

▶ Read the extract from 'Wings of a Dove' (Part 3, pages 100–101) by the Caribbean poet, Kamau Brathwaite, set in post-independence Kingston, Jamaica. The poet introduces the figure of Brother-Man, a Rastafarian, who then takes on the voice of the poem. Use the following questions to come to an initial appreciation of the poem:

- What are your first impressions? What strikes you about the style in which it was written?
- How would you describe the tone of the poem?
- What type of culture does Brathwaite identify with and how is this reflected in the language?
- How would you describe the attitude to whites and colonial culture in the poem?

Now consider the poem specifically as post-colonial literature. What would you say were its key features as post-colonial writing? How does the poem reflect key issues of its Caribbean context? How might the concepts of difference or hybridity be useful in coming to an appreciation of the poem? Do there seem any contradictions or tensions within the work?

▶ Compare 'Wings of a Dove' with an earlier Caribbean poem, 'Kinky Hair Blues' (Part 3, pages 95–96), by Una Marson:

- How does the tone and form of Marson's poem differ from Brathwaite's?
- If Brathwaite's poem can be read as confrontational, what strategies does Marson use to convey her point?
- How effective do you find the use of Creole in 'Kinky Hair Blues'?
- To what extent would you see these poems as reflecting common concerns, and to what extent would you emphasise their differences?
- Which would you say asserts a more radical distance from the colonial centre? Which, perhaps, undermines a sense of 'Other'?

Gender is an important issue when writing about post-colonial literature. How are male and female personas portrayed in the poems? How might Marson's poem be seen as a critique of both colonialism and patriarchy?

What aspects of the language of each poem would you use to support your ideas?

How to write about colonial literature

Writing about colonial literature also requires sensitivity to language and a discriminating use of critical concepts. The following passage is taken from *A Passage to India* (1924) by the English writer, E.M. Forster, and is set in the country of the title. Mr McBryde, the Superintendent of Police, is opening the case for the prosecution; it is against an Indian, Dr Aziz, who has been accused of assaulting an English woman, Miss Quested:

> Mr MacBryde was not at pains to be an interesting speaker; he left eloquence to the defence, who would require it. His attitude was, 'Everyone knows the man's guilty, and I am obliged to say so in public before he goes to the Andamans.' He made no moral or emotional appeal, and it was only by degrees that the studied negligence of his manner made itself felt, and lashed part of the audience to fury. Laboriously did he describe the genesis of the picnic. The prisoner had met Miss Quested at an entertainment given by the Principal of Government College, and had there conceived his intentions concerning her: prisoner was a man of loose life, as documents found upon him at his arrest would testify, also his fellow assistant, Dr Panna Lal, was in a position to throw light on his character, and Major Callendar himself would speak. Here Mr McBryde paused. He wanted to keep the proceedings as clean as possible, but Oriental Pathology, his favourite theme, lay all around him, and he could not resist it. Taking off his spectacles, as was his habit before enunciating a general truth, he looked into them sadly, and remarked that the darker races are physically attracted by the fairer, but not vice versa – not a matter of bitterness this, not a matter for abuse, but just a fact which any scientific observer will confirm.

▶ How would you describe the attitude of McBryde to both the case and 'the prisoner'? What aspects of this writing, concerning either the ideas conveyed or how the scene is depicted, seem particularly 'colonial'? How might the concept of 'Orientalist discourse' provide a framework for analysing this passage?

The setting of the court room (a symbol of British rule?) may have a particular significance here, as 'discourse' is concerned with how 'knowledge' is entwined with power. Consider how McBryde's sense of 'knowledge' about the prisoner and 'Oriental Pathology' seems to support his authority and enhance his sense of control. To what extent is Aziz an individual or a racial stereotype in McBryde's mind? In what ways is a sense of Indians as 'Other' developed in this scene?

Writing about English literature from a post-colonial perspective

The very fact that certain English texts can now be labelled as 'colonial' indicates the extent to which English literature can now viewed from a post-colonial perspective. This re-evaluation of English texts, from the position of historical distance, is a key aspect of writing about literature in the post-colonial world. It is part of a process of rereading and reinterpreting the English canon.

In the case of literature which explicitly depicts the colonial encounter (such as Conrad's 'Heart of Darkness' or Forster's *A Passage to India*), this can mean challenging the assumptions and validity of the text itself, or even coming to a better understanding of the workings of the colonial mind-set. It may be, as with the Forster extract, that the values reflected in writing do not necessarily reflect the beliefs of the author. Furthermore, works like 'Heart of Darkness' and *A Passage to India* are problematic because they both criticise colonialism, yet seem to maintain certain colonial assumptions.

However, another key aspect of writing about English texts from a post-colonial perspective is showing how works which may previously have been viewed as having only an incidental relationship to colonialism (such as Charlotte Brontë's *Jane Eyre* or Jane Austen's *Mansfield Park,* 1814), are actually deeply rooted in this aspect of English history (see Part 5: Edward Said's *Culture and Imperialism,* 1993, page 121). Such criticism shows an awareness of the broad geographical context of these novels and examines the significance of the colonies within the text, a significance which previous critics may have ignored.

Writing about all texts, whether those from the English canon or those that have historically been regarded as colonial or post-colonial, it is essential to bear in mind the possibilities of different readings; this may involve both an awareness of how different readings have evolved over time and an awareness of how different geographical, cultural and historical contexts shape the responses of readers. Writing about literature from a post-colonial perspective, you need to be aware not only of the context of the literature you are responding to, but also of the context which you are writing from and how that affects your own reading. It may even be important to challenge some of your own assumptions by considering how readers in other contexts might respond to the same piece of work.

Assignments

1 What does the term 'post-colonial' mean to you?

2 How important do you think a knowledge of colonialism is when approaching post-colonial texts?

3 Consider how your own background may affect your appreciation of the post-colonial texts you are studying.

4 Compare how two writers have responded to an historical event or period; for instance, Indian independence and partition in Anita Desai's *Clear Light of Day* and Salman Rushdie's *Midnight's Children*.

5 A comparative study could be made of two writers from different contexts, but who share similar concerns and styles, such as the social realist novelists, Mulk Raj Anand and C.L.R. James.

6 Work on a on a project in which you compare the styles and concerns of two women writers from different geographical regions. You could focus on the portrayal of women in Tsitsi Dangarembga's *Nervous Conditions* and Arundhati Roy's *The God of Small Things*.

7 Write a feminist critique of a text you are studying by a male post-colonial writer.

8 Decide upon a particular theme or issue within a text that you would like to do an in-depth study of, such as displacement and identity in Michael Ondaatje's *The English Patient*. Make a thorough analysis of the topic through detailed rereading of the text.

9 Make a comparative study of two texts, concentrating on one theme; for instance, attitudes to history in *The English Patient* and V.S. Naipaul's *A Bend in the River*.

10 Compare colonial and post-colonial texts which are both relevant to the same region or have a direct literary connection (such as Charlotte Brontë's *Jane Eyre* and Jean Rhys' *Wide Sargasso Sea*, or Joseph Conrad's 'Heart of Darkness' and V.S. Naipaul's *A Bend in the River*). You could discuss issues of representation and perspective and the relationship between the texts.

11 After reading the extracts from *Midnight's Children* and Ben Okri's *The Famished Road* (Part 3, pages 76–77 and pages 86–87), come to your own definition of magic realism. Write a passage using this technique: what have you learnt about the benefits and challenges of adopting this style?

12 After reading the extracts from M.R. Anand, C.L.R. James, Ngugi and Gordimer, consider what the term 'realist' means to you. Think about the different functions this kind of writing might have in a post-colonial context in general, and in the specific contexts of the authors concerned.

5 | Resources

Bibliography of texts discussed

Colonial and related texts
William Shakespeare *The Tempest* (1611)
Charlotte Brontë *Jane Eyre* (1847)
Joseph Conrad 'Heart of Darkness' (1902)
E.M. Forster *A Passage To India* (1924)

Post-colonial texts
India
Mulk Raj Anand *Untouchable* (1935; Bodley Head, 1970); *Coolie* (1936; Penguin, 1945)
R.K. Narayan *Swami and Friends* (1935) *The Bachelor of Arts* (1937) and *The English Teacher* (1945) in *A Malgudi Omnibus* (Minerva, 1994)
Raja Rao *Kanthapura* (1937; Oxford India Paperbacks, 1989)
Anita Desai *Games at Twilight and other stories* (Penguin, 1972); *Clear Light of Day* (William Heinemann, 1980); *In Custody* (William Heinemann, 1984)
Salman Rushdie *Midnight's Children* (Picador, 1982); *Shame* (Jonathan Cape,1983)
Arundhati Roy *The God of Small Things* (Flamingo, 1997)

Africa
Chinua Achebe *Things Fall Apart* (Heinemann, 1962); *No Longer At Ease* (Heinemann, 1960); *Arrow of God* (Heinemann, 1964); *A Man of the People* (Heinemann, 1966)
Wole Soyinka *A Dance of the Forests* (1960) in *Collected Plays* 1 (Oxford University Press, 1973); *The Lion and The Jewel* (1959) and *Madmen and Specialists* (1970) in *Collected Plays 2* (Oxford University Press, 1974)
Ngugi wa Thiong'o *A Grain of Wheat* (Heinemann, 1968); *Petals of Blood* (Heinemann, 1977)
Tsitsi Dangarembga *Nervous Conditions* (The Women's Press, 1988)
Ben Okri *The Famished Road* (Vintage, 1992)

South Africa
Athol Fugard *The Coat* (1966), *Sizwe Bansi is Dead* (1972) and *The Island* (1973) in *The Township Plays* (Oxford University Press, 1993)

Nadine Gordimer 'Six Feet of the Country' (1956; Penguin 1982); *Burger's Daughter* (Penguin, 1980)
J.M. Coetzee *Life and Times of Michael K* (Penguin, 1985); *Foe* (Secker and Warburg, 1986); *Disgrace* (Secker and Warburg, 1999)

The Caribbean
C.L.R. James 'Triumph' (1929), reprinted in *The Routledge Reader in Caribbean Literature* (Routledge, 1996) [see below]; *Minty Alley* (1936; New Beacon, 1975)
V.S. Reid *New Day* (Heinemann, 1949)
V.S. Naipaul *Miguel Street* (1959; Penguin 1971)
Una Marson *The Moth and The Star* (the author, Jamaica, 1937)
Louise Bennett *Selected Poems* (Sangsters Book Stores Ltd, Kingston, Jamaica, 1982)
Derek Walcott *Collected Poems 1948–1984* (Faber and Faber, 1992)
Kamau Brathwaite *Arrivants, New World Trilogy* (Oxford University Press, 1973)

Transcultural writing
V.S. Naipaul *A Bend in the River* (Penguin, 1980)
Michael Ondaatje *Running in the Family* (Picador, 1984); *The English Patient* (Picador, 1993)
Jean Rhys *Wide Sargasso Sea* (Penguin, 1968)

Further reading

Useful anthologies
James Berry, ed. *News for Babylon* (Chatto and Windus, 1984)
Excellent selection of contemporary West Indian British poetry.
Elleke Boehmer, ed. *Empire Writing, an Anthology of Colonial Literature 1870–1918* (Oxford University Press, 1998)
Contains a wide range of useful and interesting writing.
Paula Burnett, ed. *The Penguin Book of Caribbean Verse* (Penguin, 1986)
Emphasises both oral and literary traditions.
Alison Donnell and Sarah Lawson Welsh, eds. *The Routledge Reader in Caribbean Literature* (Routledge, 1996)
Criticism and literature is introduced in its cultural and political context.

Selections of essays by post-colonial authors

Chinua Achebe *Morning Yet on Creation Day: Essays* (Heinemann, 1975)
V.S. Naipaul *Finding the Centre* (Penguin, 1985)
Salman Rushdie *Imaginary Homelands* (Granta, 1992)
Ngugi wa Thiong'o *Writers in Politics* (Heinemann, 1981)

Interviews and general anthologies

Bill Ashcroft, Gareth Griffiths, Helen Tiffin, eds. *The Post-colonial Studies Reader* (Routledge, 1995)
Contains essays by writers and academics on key issues.
Feroza Jussawalla and Reed Way Dasenbrock, eds. *Interviews with Writers of the Post-colonial World* (University Press of Mississippi, 1992)
John Thieme, ed. *The Arnold Anthology of Post-colonial Literatures in English* (Arnold, 1996)
Jane Wilkinson *Talking with African Writers, Interviews by Jane Wilkinson* (James Currey and Heinemann, 1990)
Wide-ranging selection of literature and essays.

Critical introductions to post-colonial literature

Bill Ashcroft, Gareth Griffiths and Helen Tiffin *The Empire Writes Back: Theory and Practice in Post-colonial Literatures* (Routledge, 1989)
Elleke Boehmer *Colonial and Post-colonial Literature* (Oxford University Press, 1995)
Bruce King, ed. *New National and Post-colonial Literatures* (Clarendon Press, 1996)
Dennis Walder *Post-colonial Literatures in English: History, Language, Theory* (Blackwell, 1998)
Both Walder and Boehmer take a strongly contextual approach.

Influential studies on the culture of empire

Edward W. Said *Orientalism* (1978; Penguin, 1991); *Culture and Empire* (Chatto and Windus, 1993)

Introductions to post-colonial theory

Peter Childs and R.J. Patrick Williams *An Introduction to Post-colonial Theory* (Prentice Hall, Harvester Wheatsheaf, 1997)
Ania Loomba *Colonialism/Postcolonialism* (Routledge, 1998)

Introductions which focus on particular regions

Michael Chapman *Southern African Literatures* (Longman, 1996)

K.R. Srinivasa Iyengar *Indian Writing in English* (Sterling Publishers, 1962)
Particularly useful for pre-independence literature.

Bruce King, ed. *West Indian Literature* (second edition, Macmillan Educational, 1995)

Mapalive-Hangson Msiska and Paul Hyland, eds. *Writing and Africa* (Longman, 1997)

Kenneth Ramchand *An Introduction to the Study of West Indian Literature* (Thomas Nelson, 1976)

Historical and cultural background

M.E. Chamberlain *The Scramble for Africa* (Longman, 1974)
Contains an excellent extracts section.

John Darwin *Britain and Decolonisation* (Macmillan, 1988)

Richard Hart *From Occupation to Independence: a Short History of the Peoples of the English-speaking Caribbean Region* (Pluto Press, 1988)

John Iliffe *Africans: The History of a Continent* (Cambridge University Press, 1995)

Burton Stein *A History of India* (Blackwell Publishers, 1998)

Internet sites

There are many sites available on individual authors, but with varying degrees of quality and usefulness. The Internet can provide access to biographical information, reviews, interviews and discussion of particular texts.

Contemporary Post-colonial and Post-imperial literatures: an overview which gives access to a wide range of relevant information according to region:
http://landow.stg.brown.edu/post/misc/postov.html

Sites for Nobel Prize winning authors: Wole Soyinka (1986); Nadine Gordimer (1991); Derek Walcott (1992) includes biographical information and transcripts of Nobel lectures. The Home Page can found at:
http://www.nobel.se/index.html

Glossary

Allegory writing in which the meaning is both literal and beneath the surface. The deeper meaning may be understood through an interpretation of signs or symbols.

Allusion when a writer refers to another work (written or oral), author or event.

Appropriation adoption and adaptation of language or culture.

Canon selection of texts, partly for the purpose of study, regarded as exemplary. In colonial terms the canon represented an assertion of Englishness and cultural superiority.

Caste system hereditary Hindu class system, where individuals are ranked according to their supposed level of spiritual purity or pollution. Each caste is associated with specific occupations. The highest is the Brahmin caste, the priest class. The lowest group are the untouchables, so called because it was believed that their occupations, such as cleaning latrines or leather working, made them polluted.

Cultural signifier a sign, whether word or object, which represents or refers to an area of culture, the meaning of the sign to be understood within its linguistic and cultural context.

Diaspora dispersion or mass migration of a people or race.

Difference on a cultural level, the assertion of distinctiveness in relation to others.

Discourse the system by which knowledge of a particular field is organised and the subject is constructed. Such 'knowledge' is produced from a position of dominance and supports the prejudices and assumptions of the dominant group.

Dramatic monologue a poem in which the poet adopts the persona of an imaginary speaker, who addresses an audience other than the reader alone. The character unwittingly reveals aspects of his/her character, beliefs, etc.

Empowerment gaining of power, authority, confidence, redressing the denigration caused by colonialism.

Gender/feminist writing awareness of the distinctive purpose, perspective and traditions of male and female writing and how what is regarded as male or female is constructed culturally. Feminist writing represents women's experience from a female perspective and is critical of patriarchy. Its purpose has been to counteract the stereotyping and marginality of women in male writing.

Hegemony the means, generally cultural, by which the ruling group come to dominate without direct oppression.

Hybridity the creation of a new form from previously distinct elements; mixed, eclectic, mongrel. The disintegration of notions of fixed or pure forms of culture.

Indigenous native, existing before colonisation.

Magic realism fiction characterised by a strongly fantastical element (often drawing on mythology or fairytale) juxtaposed with everyday, historical reality. Such fiction often contains labyrinthine plots and multiple worlds.

Marginality existence at the periphery, exclusion from the centre.

Marxism philosophy based on the writings of Karl Marx (1818-1883). Marx emphasised seeing the individual in terms of the material, historical and economic forces that shape his/her experience and perception. Marxist writers often represent characters within social and economic forces and see their purpose as raising the consciousness of their readers and exposing the illusory or oppressive nature of the dominant ideology. Ideology can mean a set of political beliefs, but, more subtlety, the ways in which the values of a society's dominant class unconsciously influence perception throughout society. As with discourse, ideology emphasises how values and perception are bound up with social and political structures.

Metropolis the centre of empire, source of the dominating culture.

Negritude cultural and literary movement of black writers which sought to reclaim an African heritage and counteract the negative stereotyping of colonialism. Mainly active in former French colonies, it has been influential throughout America, the Caribbean and Africa. Though important for celebrating African culture, it can be criticised for itself romanticising and stereotyping Africans and their past.

Otherness construction and representation of colonial peoples and places as Other, removed and subordinate to the metropolis.

Pastiche writing in deliberate imitation of another's style.

Patriarchy male dominance which disempowers or marginalises women.

Persona the imagined character and voice adopted by an author, particularly in poetry.

Realism seeking to reflect the material, historical world in fiction. Realist writing often concentrates upon the relationship of characters to society, its values and influence.

Representation how individuals, peoples or historical events are portrayed. No representation is ever neutral; writing is not a mirror which reflects the world, but a means through which it is constructed. In a post-colonial context, representation is linked to issues of bias, stereotyping and the influence of discourse.

Stereotype representation of an individual in terms of the prejudices of the observer; the individual is seen as a simplified type rather then a complex human being. Because stereotyping does not recognise individual thoughts/feelings it also dehumanises and creates a sense of Other.

Transcultural writing which crosses cultural and geographical boundaries, often the product of diaspora.

Index

Acknowledgements

The author and publishers wish to thank the following for permission to use copyright material:

Gillon Aitken Associates Ltd on behalf of the author for extracts from V.S. Naipaul *Miguel Street*, Penguin (1971) pp. 84–85. Copyright © 1959 by V.S. Naipaul; and V.S. Naipaul *A Bend in the River*, Penguin (1980) pp. 14, 17, 238, 276–277. Copyright © 1979 by V.S. Naipaul; Mulk Raj Anand for a extract from his book *Coolie*, Penguin World Classics (1936) p. 216; Faber and Faber Ltd and Farrar, Straus and Giroux, LLC for extracts from Derek Walcott 'The Schooner Flight', 'A Far Cry from Africa' and 'A Simple Flame, Part IV' from *Collected Poems 1948–1984* by Derek Walcott. Copyright © 1986 by Derek Walcott; David Godwin Associates on behalf of the author for an extract from Ben Okri *The Famished Road*, Vintage (1991) pp. 476–478; HarperCollins Publishers Ltd and David Godwin Associates on behalf of the author for extracts from Arundhati Roy *God of Small Things*, Flamingo (1997) pp. 31, 126–127; Heinemann Educational Publishers, a division of Reed Educational & Professional Publishing Ltd, for extracts from Chinua Achebe *Things Fall Apart* (1958) pp. 5–6; and Ngugi wa Thiong'o *A Grain of Wheat* (1968) pp. 111–112; David Higham Associates Ltd on behalf of the author for extracts from J.M. Coetzee *The Life and Times of Michael K*, Secker & Warburg (1983) pp. 140, 183–184, 185; and J.M. Coetzee *Disgrace*, Secker & Warburg (1999) pp. 158, 216; Alfred A Knopf, Inc, a division of Random House Inc and Laurence Pollinger Ltd on behalf of the author for an extract from Victor Stafford Reid *New Day*, p.191–192. Copyright © 1949 by Alfred A Knopf Inc; Methuen Publishing Ltd and Hill and Wang, a division of Farrar, Straus and Giroux LLC for an extract from Wole Soyinka *Madman and Specialists*. Copyright © 1971, renewed 1999 by Wole Soyinka; New Beacon Books for extracts from C.L.R. James *Minty Alley* (1936), New Beacon Books (1975) pp. 125–126, and James Berry 'Lucy's Letter' from *Lucy's Letter and Loving* by James Berry (1982); Oxford University Press for extracts from Athol Fugard 'The Coat' from *Township Plays* (1993) pp. 178–180. Copyright © Athol Fugard 1967; and Kamau Brathwaite 'Atumpan' and 'Wings of a Dove' from *The Arrivants: A New World Trilogy* by Kamau Brathwaite (1973); and Wole Soyinka *A Dance of the Forests* from *Collected Plays 1* (1963) pp. 60–61 and *The Lion and The Jewel* from *Collected Plays 2* (1963) pp. 8–9; Oxford University Press, New Delhi, India for an extract from Raja Rao *Kanthapura* (1937), Oxford India Paperbacks (1989) pp. 88–89; Random House UK with the Wallace Literary Agency, Inc on behalf of the author for extracts from R.K. Narayan 'The Bachelor of Arts', pp. 218–219. Copyright © 1937 by R.K. Narayan, and R.K. Narayan 'The English Teacher', pp. 467–468. Copyright © 1945 by R.K. Narayan; and with Knopf Canada, a division of Random House of Canada Ltd, for extracts from Salman Rushdie *Midnight's Children*, pp. 227, 432, 439–440. Copyright © 1981 by Salman Rushdie; Rogers, Coleridge & White Ltd on behalf of the author for extracts from Anita Desai *In Custody*, William Heinemann (1984) pp. 42–43, 193–194. Copyright © Anita Desai 1984; and Anita Desai 'Games at Twilight' from *Games at Twilight* by Anita Desai, William Heinemann (1978) p. 72. Copyright © Anita Desai 1978; Viking Penguin, a division of Penguin Putnam Inc, and A.P. Watt Ltd on behalf of the author for extracts from Nadine Gordimer *Burger's Daughter*, Penguin (1980) pp. 163, 142–143. Copyright © 1979 by Nadine Gordimer.

Every effort has been made to reach copyright holders; the publishers would like to hear from anyone whose rights they have unknowingly infringed.